THE
NORMANDY
LANDINGS

D-DAY

The Invasion of Europe 6 June 1944

THE NORMANDY LANDINGS

D-DAY

The Invasion of Europe 6 June 1944

DEREK BLIZARD

Old men forget; yet all shall be forgot,
But he'll remember with advantages
What feats he did that day.

WILLIAM SHAKESPEARE, *HENRY V*, ACT IV SCENE III

TO MY FATHER WHO FOUGHT IN THE FIRST ONE

THE NORMANDY LANDINGS

First published in 1993 by Hamlyn,
an imprint of Octopus Publishing Group Ltd

This edition published 2004 by Bounty Books,
an imprint of Octopus Publishing Group Ltd,
2-4 Heron Quays, London E14 4JP

Reprinted 2004

Designers: William Mason, Vivienne Cherry
Picture Research: Jenny Faithfull, Anne Hobart
Production: Michelle Thomas, Sarah Coltman

Executive Editors: Sarah Polden, Lesley McOwan
Art Director: Tim Foster

Copyright © 1993 Octopus Publishing Group Ltd

ISBN 0 7537 0904 X

A CIP catalogue record for this book is available from the British Library

Typeset in Sabon by Servis Filmsetting, Manchester, England
Colour reproduction by Mandarin Offset, Hong Kong
Produced by Toppan Printing Co, (HK) Ltd
Printed and bound in Hong Kong

*Previous pages: Arromanches and the famous MULBERRY harbour
60 years on; OMAHA beach as it is today*

CONTENTS

Foreword to the 1st edition

BY THE LATE SIR JOHN MOGG, GCB CBE DSO DL

This book has been published to commemorate the 60th Anniversary of D-Day and the start of the Normandy Campaign.

On 6 June the Allied Expeditionary Force embarked on the greatest amphibious military operation in the history of warfare, involving hundreds of thousands of men, huge flotillas of ships and landing craft and massive air support.

This Crusade of the Allied forces was aimed at the destruction of the German War Machine, the elimination of Nazi tyranny and the reversal of the evil suppression of the peoples of Europe.

It was an immensely proud moment for me, as a very tiny cog in the huge Allied machine, to be asked to write a foreword to this extremely valuable book. As the first President of the Normandy Veterans Association I know how much the Veterans, whose memories may fade, like mine, will appreciate this timely reminder of the events leading to the successful conclusion of the Normandy Campaign. Those who have come after and benefited from the freedom and peace will learn a great deal from this vivid account of a remarkable enterprise.

Derek Blizard has carried out much dedicated research in producing this book and has put it together in an uncomplicated, concise style, well supported by fascinating photographs and informative maps. He has produced a historic record for which many people, both young and old, will be grateful.

He analyzes the vast and detailed planning commitment which started in 1940 when Britain stood alone. He goes on to describe the formidable task facing the Allies and the build up of troops in Britain from the United States and Canada, and eventually from the occupied countries of Europe including Free-French, Polish, Czech, Belgian, Dutch and Norwegian forces. He vividly presents the personalities and thoughts of the Allied Senior Commanders, and the difficulties of welding them into a team.

With an operation of this magnitude and importance, such areas as security, deception plans and appropriate weapons and equipment were central to success; all these points are discussed. But the book emphasizes that, however good the plans, the weapons, equipment and training, the most important factor is always the *man* and not the machine. The man who does the right thing at the right time with the right courage and the right spirit and belief in his cause is the key to success.

It was serving men and women, supported by the civilians in factories and war industries, who achieved the historic feat of destroying Hitler's Third Reich, freeing Europe from the evil tyranny of Nazi oppression. Sometimes, when all these men and women remember what they endured in good moments and bad (and some were very bad), let them also recall how much they achieved, how great was their effort and their comradeship and particularly how much we all owe to those who never returned.

A debt of gratitude is due to the author and the individuals who have produced this book for collating the events, the stories and

Left: General Montgomery presenting Lieutenant Colonel John Mogg with the DSO at Creully on 14 June 1944 after the battle of Lingèvres, near Tilly-sur-Seulles, when he was commanding the 9th Battalion of the Durham Light Infantry.

experiences of those who took part in the victorious and liberating march starting from the Normandy beaches, a march described by Winston Churchill as 'unsurpassed through all the story of war'.

I hope that all who read this book will be inspired by the example and proud achievement of those whom it portrays.

SUPREME HEADQUARTERS
ALLIED EXPEDITIONARY FORCE

Soldiers, Sailors and Airmen of the Allied Expeditionary Force!

You are about to embark upon the Great Crusade, toward which we have striven these many months. The eyes of the world are upon you. The hopes and prayers of liberty-loving people everywhere march with you. In company with our brave Allies and brothers-in-arms on other Fronts, you will bring about the destruction of the German war machine, the elimination of Nazi tyranny over the oppressed peoples of Europe, and security for ourselves in a free world.

Your task will not be an easy one. Your enemy is well trained, well equipped and battle-hardened. He will fight savagely.

But this is the year 1944! Much has happened since the Nazi triumphs of 1940-41. The United Nations have inflicted upon the Germans great defeats, in open battle, man-to-man. Our air offensive has seriously reduced their strength in the air and their capacity to wage war on the ground. Our Home Fronts have given us an overwhelming superiority in weapons and munitions of war, and placed at our disposal great reserves of trained fighting men. The tide has turned! The free men of the world are marching together to Victory!

I have full confidence in your courage, devotion to duty and skill in battle. We will accept nothing less than full Victory!

Good Luck! And let us all beseech the blessing of Almighty God upon this great and noble undertaking.

Dwight Eisenhower

Left: The Great Crusade. General Eisenhower's inspiring message to the Allied forces on the eve of the Normandy invasion.

Right: Confidence abounds in the message sent by General Montgomery, Commander-in-Chief Allied ground forces.

*B. L. Montgomery
General*

21 ARMY GROUP

PERSONAL MESSAGE
FROM THE C-in-C

To be read out to all Troops

1. The time has come to deal the enemy a terrific blow in Western Europe.

The blow will be struck by the combined sea, land, and air forces of the Allies—together constituting one great Allied team, under the supreme command of General Eisenhower.

2. On the eve of this great adventure I send my best wishes to every soldier in the Allied team.

To us is given the honour of striking a blow for freedom which will live in history; and in the better days that lie ahead men will speak with pride of our doings. We have a great and a righteous cause.

Let us pray that " The Lord Mighty in Battle " will go forth with our armies, and that His special providence will aid us in the struggle.

3. I want every soldier to know that I have complete confidence in the successful outcome of the operations that we are now about to begin.

With stout hearts, and with enthusiasm for the contest, let us go forward to victory.

4. And, as we enter the battle, let us recall the words of a famous soldier spoken many years ago :—

> *" He either fears his fate too much,*
> *Or his deserts are small,*
> *Who dare not put it to the touch,*
> *To win or lose it all."*

5. Good luck to each one of you. And good hunting on the mainland of Europe.

*B. L. Montgomery
General
C-in-C 21 Army Group.*

5 - 6 - 1944.

CHAPTER ONE

Prelude to Invasion

Above: War on the Eastern front. Soviet troops leap from their trenches to attack German positions during the counter-offensive of 1944.

NOVEMBER 1942

EL ALAMEIN

As the year 1944 dawned it was clear that the tide of war was running against Nazi Germany. After more than four years of fighting, during which their conquests had reached from the Pyrenees to the Volga and from Norway to the edge of the Nile Delta, Hitler's armies were everywhere on the defensive. The turning point had come in November 1942 when General Bernard Montgomery led the British 8th Army to a decisive victory over the combined German and Italian Desert Army at El Alamein in Egypt, so ending the German threat to Cairo and the Suez Canal. The enemy forces were swept out of Egypt and the Italian protectorate of Libya and driven across the border into Tunisia, which was then controlled by the Vichy puppet government that had been established in unoccupied France.

Shortly after this defeat, Hitler and his Italian allies suffered another surprise blow. British and American troops, sailing direct from Britain and from the United States, carried out the Operation TORCH landings in Morocco and Algeria which, like Tunisia, were under the control of Vichy France. The retreating German and Italian forces in Tunisia were thus squarely caught between a

TORCH

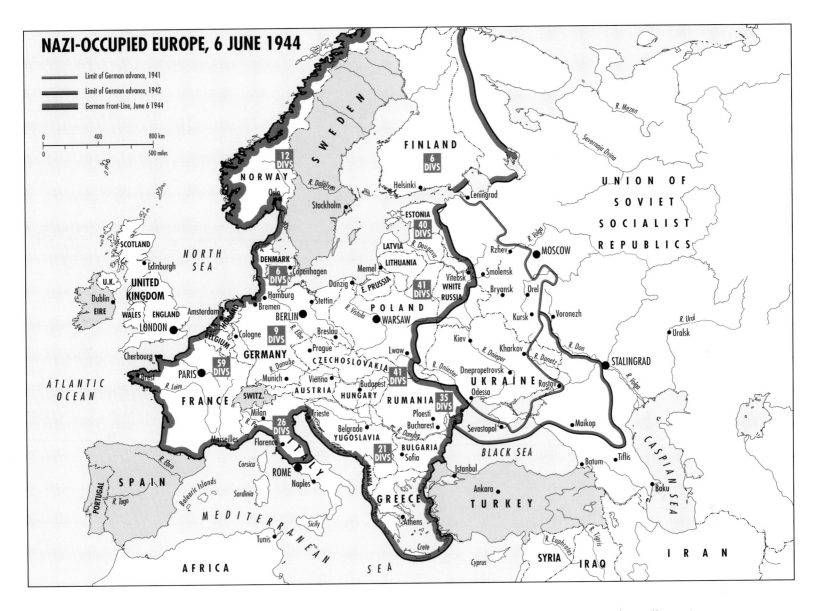

NAZI-OCCUPIED EUROPE, 6 JUNE 1944

Limit of German advance, 1941
Limit of German advance, 1942
German Front-Line, June 6 1944

British-American army moving eastwards from Algeria and Montgomery's 8th Army advancing north from Libya. Hitler's response to this Allied threat was simultaneously to occupy the rest of France and to rush German reinforcements by air and sea from Sicily into Tunisia. The move, however, was to cost him dear. By May 1943, after savage fighting, the Germans and Italians were trapped in the Cape Bon peninsula near Tunis and were forced to surrender. For the German High Command it was a disaster. Not only had German forces been driven out of North Africa, but the Tunisian campaign

MAY 1943

had cost them nearly a quarter of a million troops, including some of their elite divisions.

The Allied victory in North Africa at once exposed what the British Prime Minister, Winston Churchill, described as the 'soft underbelly' of Nazi dominated Europe: the northern shores of the Mediterranean. Following on their success, the British and Americans wasted little time in preparing to invade Sicily, where more than 400,000 Allied troops were put ashore in July 1943. The Sicilian landings amounted to a massive air and naval operation – an important exercise in cooperation between the Western Allies

SICILY: JULY 1943

Left: German defeat at Stalingrad. The tattered, half-frozen remnants of General Von Paulus's 6th Army march into captivity under the watchful eye of Soviet troops, January 1943. Stalingrad marked the watershed of Hitler's invasion of Russia.

AUGUST 1943

and one that provided crucial lessons for the even greater invasion that ultimately lay ahead. By the end of August 1943 Sicily had been cleared of the enemy, and on 3 September the British 8th Army crossed the Straits of Messina onto the mainland of Italy. Six days later the Anglo-American 5th Army under the command of US General Mark Clark began landing at Salerno, just south of

ITALY SURRENDERS

Naples. Within hours the Italian government capitulated to the Allies.

While these momentous events were taking place in the Mediterranean, the Germans were suffering an even greater military setback on the Eastern Front. Operation BARBAROSSA – the *Wehrmacht*'s invasion of Soviet Russia – which began in June 1941, finally ground to a halt in November 1942 in

STALINGRAD

the battle for the key city of Stalingrad on the River Volga. The Red Army, in a brilliant counterstroke, brought reinforcements secretly across the frozen river, eventually

trapping General Friedrich von Paulus's 6th Army inside the ruins of the city. At the end of January 1943 von Paulus surrendered. The Germans lost more than 100,000 killed while some 90,000 troops were taken prisoner, among them 24 generals.

Stalingrad signalled the final destruction of Hitler's hopes of conquering Russia. The Russians launched a counteroffensive along the 3,200-km (2,000-mile) front that extended across European Russia from the Arctic Sea to the Caucasus. Throughout 1943 the Soviet armies, drawing on seemingly limitless manpower reserves and strengthened by a flood of supplies and equipment that began to reach them from the United States and Britain, relentlessly drove the German invaders back. By the spring of 1944 they had advanced to a line that ran from the Gulf of Finland through Belorussia, into Poland as far as Lvov and along the River Dniester to the Black Sea near Odessa. Almost the whole of the Ukraine was

RUSSIAN COUNTEROFFENSIVE

SPRING 1944

Left: The Allied landing at Anzio, south of Rome, January 1944. American driven DUKW amphibious trucks carry British infantry ashore. In spite of strenuous efforts by the Allies, Rome was not taken until 4 June 1944.

back in Soviet hands, but the German armies, though outnumbered and battle weary, remained a powerful fighting force.

Meanwhile, in the West, the Allied advance in Italy had been checked. The British-American forces had become bogged down on the Gustav Line, which ran along the Garigliano and Sangro rivers north of Naples. The Germans, skilfully commanded by Field Marshal Kesselring, were successfully holding up some twenty Allied divisions, denying all their attempts to capture the key stronghold of Monte Cassino. Frustration was reaching boiling point and the Allied leaders were becoming thoroughly dismayed. Most of continental Europe, including France,

Left: Italy, April 1944. German paratroopers well concealed among the ruins of the hilltop monastery of Monte Cassino. The Germans fought tenaciously to hold this mountain stronghold and were not finally dislodged until 18 May.

Above: Italy, March 1944. Allied artillery bombarding the town of Cassino at the foot of the hills beneath the great monastery, part of which can be seen top right.

Belgium, Holland, Norway, Denmark and the Balkans, still lay firmly in German hands, and it was clear that a narrow frontal assault in Italy across difficult mountain terrain was not going to break the deadlock that existed in western Europe.

This, then, was the situation that the Western Allies faced in the spring of 1944. And it lent new urgency to the great enterprise that they had been secretly preparing: the opening of a second front on the mainland of Europe.

CHAPTER TWO

A Second Front

The idea of opening a second front against the Germans in Europe had been under discussion for some time. Even as early as 1940, when they stood alone against Hitler after the disasters of the evacuation from Dunkirk and the collapse of France, the British had begun to plan for the day when they would recross the English Channel. In their hearts they knew that the war could only ultimately be won by striking at Germany through France. To this end they began training elite commando units to carry out raids on the enemy held coast. However, even their defiant spirit could not alter the fact that, with their forces strung out across the globe from the North Atlantic to Singapore, the British simply did not have sufficient strength to tackle the might of the German Army head on.

The situation changed dramatically with the entry of the United States into the war in December 1941. Japan's surprise attack on the American fleet at Pearl Harbor in Hawaii galvanized the American nation. A few days later Nazi Germany too – in a move of incalculable recklessness – declared war upon the United States. At a stroke the entire strategic position was transformed and the implications for Great Britain as well as for the struggling Soviet Union were immense. The vast industrial and military potential of America would at last be unleashed. Britain could now count on American help on a scale that Winston Churchill had long dreamed of. At the Washington conference in late December 1941 the British Prime Minister

and the United States President, Franklin D. Roosevelt, agreed on a grand strategy for achieving victory. They decided to concentrate all their efforts first on the defeat of Nazi Germany while fighting what amounted to a war of containment only against Japan.

The 'Germany first' decision proved to be one of the most significant in the history of World War II, although Roosevelt had to overcome bitter opposition from many sections in Washington. The US Navy in particular was understandably keen to put a greater priority on defeating Japan than on striking at Germany. However, the Western leaders recognized the urgent need to confront the Germans in order to take the pressure off the Russians who, at the time, were fighting the Germans on the ground virtually unaided. Were they to be forced out of the war, the full might of Hitler's armies could be turned against the West. If that were to happen, the prospects for the British and Americans in attempting the liberation of Europe would be slim indeed.

During 1942, therefore, calls for the opening of a second front began to grow in volume. They were reinforced by mounting diplomatic pressure from Marshal Joseph Stalin. The Soviet leader, desperate to secure some relief for his hard pressed armies, scathingly asked Churchill: 'Are you going to let us do all the work while you look on? Are you never going to start fighting?' The taunt understandably annoyed the British Prime Minister, who was unable to make Stalin understand the enormity of the task that

DUNKIRK

PEARL HARBOR

WASHINGTON
CONFERENCE

STALIN

Right: The Soviet leader Joseph Stalin, President Roosevelt and the British Prime Minister Winston Churchill at the Teheran Conference, November 1943. Visible behind them are (left to right) General Arnold, Chief of US Army Air Force, General Sir Alan Brooke, Chief of the British Imperial General Staff, Admiral Cunningham, Royal Navy, and Admiral Leahy, Chief of Staff to President Roosevelt.

faced the British and Americans. Both Western powers were experiencing grave setbacks in Burma and the Pacific at the hands of the Japanese. At the same time Allied merchant shipping losses through U-boat sinkings in the North Atlantic were beginning to reach crisis point. The transatlantic convoys were Britain's lifeline. Without a steady flow of supplies her ability to continue to wage war would be seriously threatened. No-one realized more clearly than the British the impossibility of mounting a cross-Channel invasion in 1942 at a time when American strength in Britain was only just starting to

build up. At Britain's insistence, therefore, the Western Allies opted instead for the strategy of driving the Germans and their Italian allies out of North Africa before attempting such a risky operation as a direct assault on France.

British misgivings about the chances of success of a cross-Channel invasion were amply confirmed by a large scale raid in August 1942 on the French Channel port of Dieppe. The Dieppe raid was designed as a 'reconnaissance in force' to test the strength of the German defences as well as to gain experience in coordinating sea, land and air

NORTH AFRICA

THE DIEPPE RAID

forces in a combined operation. More than 6,000 troops, a large proportion of whom were Canadian, were taken in assault craft the 110 km (70 miles) from the English south coast to the beaches outside the strongly fortified French town. The raid was a disaster. Although British commandos succeeded in climbing the cliffs to knock out the German coastal batteries, they failed to prevent the Germans from directing a withering fire onto the beaches where the main landings were being made. All 30 of the new Churchill tanks that were landed were destroyed on the beach, and the Canadians and British suffered exceptionally heavy casualties: more than 3,500 men were either killed or taken prisoner. The attacking force did not even penetrate the Dieppe defences. The Canadian 2nd Division, which bore the brunt of the losses, was reduced to a tiny rump by the end of the operation.

Although frankly admitted to be a costly failure, the Dieppe raid nonetheless provided some useful lessons for the Allies. It showed first of all that no major port could be seized quickly if held by a well entrenched and determined enemy. Even more important, it showed the need for close artillery and tank support for the troops disembarking on the beaches. Dieppe made it clear that air and sea bombardment was not in itself enough to knock out the enemy fortifications in advance of the landings. This led the British to start developing specialized amphibious armour, which was later to play a very important role.

One of the most serious consequences of the Dieppe fiasco, however, was the damaging psychological effect it had upon Churchill. The Prime Minister had never recovered from the nightmare of the Gallipoli disaster against the Turks in World War I, for which he had always felt partly responsible. The Dieppe raid awakened his old fears that a cross-Channel invasion might turn out to be a similar bloodbath. His enthusiasm for such

Robert Barr of the BBC with British Paratroops on the eve of D-Day, broadcast on 6 June 1944

Their faces were darkened with cocoa; sheathed knives were strapped to their ankles; tommy guns strapped to their waists; bandoliers and hand grenades, coils of rope, pick handles, spades, rubber dinghies hung around them, and a few personal elements, like the lad who was taking a newspaper to read on the plane. I watched them march in a long, snaking, double line, almost a mile long, to draw their parachutes. Later, I saw them gathered around their CV47 aircraft and making final adjustments to their kit before they started. There was an easy familiar touch about the way they were getting ready as if they had done it often before. Well, yes, they had kitted up and climbed aboard often just like this – twenty, thirty, forty times some of them. But it had never been quite like this before. This was the first combat jump for every one of them.

an operation was thereafter always tinged with doubt. The Chief of Britain's Imperial General Staff, General Sir Alan Brooke, shared the Prime Minister's concern.

In spite of British misgivings, the Americans were determined that a full-scale assault against the Continent should take place in 1944. And early in 1943 an Anglo-American team was set up to plan such an invasion, which was given the code name Operation OVERLORD. The man chosen to head the planning team was a senior British officer, Lieutenant General Frederick Morgan. He was given the rather awkward title of Chief of Staff to the Supreme Allied Commander (designate), shortened eventually to its initials COSSAC. At the time, however, no Supreme Allied Commander had been appointed. Morgan, his American deputy, Major-General Ray Barker, and their staff were therefore on their own. Setting up their headquarters at Norfolk House in London's

Left: Dead and wounded on the beach beside a disabled British Churchill tank after the raid. The Dieppe fiasco brought home to the Allies the immensity of the task that faced them in trying to penetrate the Atlantic Wall.

OVERLORD

COSSAC

Left: Canadian troops being marched into captivity through the streets of Dieppe following the unsuccessful raid on the French port. The Canadian 2nd Division lost more than 900 men killed and hundreds more taken prisoner during the day-long battle.

St James's Square near Piccadilly, the COSSAC team got down to work.

By August 1943 Morgan and his team had come up with a plan which they presented to the combined British and American Chiefs of Staff at the Quebec Conference. The combined Chiefs in turn submitted it to Churchill and Roosevelt, who accepted it. Although the plan was to undergo major revisions and modifications later, the basic objective was to remain. Morgan proposed that the Allies should invade Normandy, the historic region of northern France lying between the ports of Le Havre in the east and Cherbourg in the west. The most obvious place to invade was the Pas-de-Calais, the part of France only 35 km (22 miles) from the English coast at Dover. Normandy, between 145 and 160 km (90 and 100 miles) from Britain, was chosen precisely because it was an area where the Germans would be least likely to expect a landing. It had a number of other advantages which Morgan spelled out: first, it was less heavily defended than the Pas-de-Calais;

second, it had good beaches, which were sheltered from the prevailing westerly winds; and, third, it offered suitable terrain for building airfields, which would be vital for the Allies to maintain air cover over the battle front. In addition, COSSAC considered that the hinterland would prove unfavourable for German armoured counterattack. The Americans, who at first favoured a landing in the Calais region, were finally persuaded that it was too great a risk in view of the strength of the German defences. An invasion of the Atlantic coast of France along the Bay of Biscay was similarly ruled out because it lay beyond range of Allied air support.

The Quebec Conference set the seal on the invasion and agreed it should take place in May the following year. At the Teheran Conference with Stalin in November 1943 Churchill and Roosevelt informed the Soviet leader of their intentions. Stalin was enthusiastic. The Red Army, he assured them, would launch a simultaneous offensive. From that moment Operation OVERLORD was under way.

AUGUST 1943

QUEBEC CONFERENCE

NORMANDY

Right: British Commandos disembark in Newhaven after returning from the disastrous Dieppe raid, August 1942. The raid was the first major combined operation to be carried out against the French Channel coast and yielded useful lessons for the D-Day invasion two years later.

TEHERAN CONFERENCE

CHAPTER THREE

Hitler's Atlantic Wall

'FORTRESS EUROPE'

The Germans had realized as long ago as December 1941 that what they called their 'Fortress Europe' was vulnerable to attack from the West. While the bulk of their army was battling against the Russians on the Eastern Front, they still had to defend a coastline that ran from the north of Norway along the shores of Denmark and the Low Countries as far as the French border with Spain. Later, the Mediterranean coast of France would also be included. Altogether it extended nearly 4,800 km (3,000 miles).

Hitler was determined to make his Fortress Europe impregnable to assault and in 1942 he ordered the construction of what became known as the Atlantic Wall. The Wall amounted to a chain of massive fortifications strung out from the Netherlands along the English Channel to the Atlantic coast of France. These fortifications comprised a wide range of structures – concrete emplacements for heavy coastal guns, underground bunkers

for troops, pillboxes bristling with heavy machine guns and antitank weapons. For two years, the construction work went ahead at frantic speed. More than 13 million cu m (460 million cu ft) of concrete and over a million tonnes (tons) of steel were used in the project, which involved the labour of thousands of foreign slave workers conscripted from all over Nazi occupied Europe. Hitler, it was later revealed, personally designed many of the features of the installations. By the time it was completed early in 1944 the Atlantic Wall constituted probably the most formidable coastal defence system ever created. The guns were almost all positioned close to the shore so that they could saturate the beaches with concentrated fire. The Germans also made sure that all ports would be particularly heavily defended, as they realized that the rapid seizure of port facilities would be essential to any invader. Along the French Channel coast from Dunkirk to Brest every seaside town, every hamlet, had been turned into a defensive strongpoint.

In spite of the work and ingenuity lavished upon it, the Atlantic Wall was certainly not impregnable. The first to appreciate this fact was one of Hitler's most experienced and capable generals, Field Marshal Erwin Rommel. Rommel had earlier commanded Germany's *Afrika Korps* in the Western Desert, where his mastery of desert warfare had made him a thorn in the side of the British from 1941 to 1943. His tactical astuteness combined with his brilliance in the handling of armoured formations on difficult terrain had

Left: One of the massive concrete gun emplacements built along the French coast. This one was located at GOLD beach in what was to be the British invasion sector. These blockhouses in many cases proved immune to both aerial and naval bombardment.

ROMMEL

become a legend and earned him the very fitting nickname the 'Desert Fox'.

Late in 1943 Hitler appointed his dashing, self-confident Field Marshal to carry out a detailed inspection of the Atlantic Wall defences. But the report that Rommel sent back came as something of a shock to the *Führer*. Rommel was strongly critical of the anti-invasion preparations made by Field Marshal von Rundstedt, the German Commander-in-Chief in the west. Von Rundstedt was an officer of the old school. He had little faith in his Atlantic Wall fortifications which he felt were too static and outmoded. He believed instead in the policy of concentrating his forces at what he considered to be the most vulnerable sections of the coast, especially around Calais which he thought was the most obvious place for the Allies to invade. At the same time he planned to keep a strong mobile force, including his key panzer (armoured) divisions, in reserve well inland.

VON RUNDSTEDT

Rommel fundamentally disagreed with this strategy. The Desert Fox firmly believed that there was only one way to defeat an invasion: to throw the enemy back into the sea at the outset. For Rommel the beaches were the critical sector. He wanted the immediate shore defences strengthened so that the invaders, if they came, would be denied any chance of obtaining a foothold, and he wanted panzer divisions stationed close behind the beaches to smash the enemy before they could properly get ashore.

It was not long before Rommel got his opportunity. Hitler placed him in command of Army Group B, which was responsible for the most important stretch of the likely invasion coast – that is from the Netherlands to Brittany. This, of course, included Normandy. The southern half of France was defended by Army Group G under the control of General Johannes Blaskowitz. Von Rundstedt remained in overall command of both

Below: Atlantic Wall defences along the French coast. These poles with mines attached were covered at high tide and designed to wreak havoc with any attempted landing. They were given the nickname 'Rommel's asparagus'.

Winston Churchill, addressing the House of Commons, 6 June 1944

The battle will grow constantly in scale and intensity for many weeks to come. I shall not attempt to speculate upon its course, but this I may say, that complete unity exists throughout the Allied armies. There is a brother-hood in arms between us and our friends of the United States. There is complete confidence in the Supreme Commander, General Eisenhower, and his lieutenants. And also in the commander of the Expeditionary Force, General Montgomery. The ardour and spirit of the troops, as I saw for myself as they were embarking in the last few days, was splendid to witness. Nothing that equipment or science can do has been neglected. And the whole process of opening the new front will be pursued with the utmost resolution both by the commanders and by the United States and British goverments whom they serve.

army groups, which together totalled 57 divisions, later increased to 59.

Rommel immediately began to put his ideas into effect. During the opening months of 1944 he tramped tirelessly around the French Channel coast, gingering up his troops and impressing everyone with his energy, thoroughness and powers of improvisation. In just a few months he managed to oversee the laying of 4 million mines, setting them with maximum density around all coastal strongpoints. He set about blocking off huge stretches of coastline with underwater obstacles of wicked ingenuity. Mines were sunk in shallow water off the beaches with lines attached to their horns. Other lethal devices were concealed on the seabed just above low water mark and were intended to rip open the bottoms of landing craft or disembarking tanks. Jagged steel girders in crisscross pattern, known as 'hedgehogs', were fixed in the sands. There were logs loaded with spikes and mines. There were so-called 'nutcracker' mines set in blocks of concrete. There were shells which could be set off by concealed tripwires. There were concrete 'dragon's teeth'. And this devilish array of obstacles was not the only deterrent.

Right: The Atlantic Wall. A well protected machine gun emplacement on the French Channel coast. Nazi troops keep a careful watch seawards for any sign of an Allied invasion.

FLOODING

Further inshore – especially in Normandy and the southern part of the Cotentin (Cherbourg) peninsula – large areas of land were deliberately flooded to prevent airborne landings and to make it difficult for an invading force to gain exit from the landing beaches.

The changes that Rommel managed to implement in a very short space of time were astonishing. It was his intention, as it was Hitler's, to inflict upon the Americans and British a military defeat that would throw them into permanent confusion and eliminate for ever the threat of an invasion in the west. Early in 1944 Rommel told his officers that they must bring their defences up to such a standard that they would be able to repel the strongest attacks. 'The enemy must be wiped out before he reaches our main battlefield', Rommel declared emphatically. 'We must stop him in the water'.

But in spite of all his efforts Rommel was not able to achieve his most important aim. He failed to persuade Hitler and von Rundstedt to give him control over their most powerful defensive weapon – the ten panzer divisions the German Army had stationed in the west. Although Hitler personally approved of Rommel's idea of keeping the panzers close to the coast, he could not afford to allow the dispute between his generals over the matter to get out of hand. He therefore decided to put a part of the panzer divisions under his own personal control, a decision that was to have important consequences. Three panzer divisions were located south of the River Loire as part of Army Group G. Two were sited in Belgium and southern Holland. The remaining five were stationed north and to the west of Paris. But none was moved to the vicinity of the Channel coast as Rommel wanted. And this was to prove crucial when invasion ultimately came.

PANZERS

CHAPTER FOUR

Britain – The Springboard

After the collapse of France in June 1940 Britain's ability to survive as a free nation was seriously in doubt. It was true that much of her small, trained front-line army had, miraculously, been rescued and brought home across the Channel from the beaches of Dunkirk, but it was an army that no longer resembled an effective fighting force. Most of its weapons and vehicles had been lost. The troops that had experienced the full shock of Nazi '*blitzkrieg*' in France and Belgium were exhausted and bewildered. In the early summer of 1940 the British had

barely enough rifles and munitions to mount a coherent defence if the Germans invaded. They could scarcely scrape together enough tanks to make up a single armoured division. Standing now alone against the might of a triumphant Nazi Germany, Britain was staring defeat in the face. Militarily her position seemed hopeless. It could only be a question of time before she was forced to sue for peace.

The inspirational leadership of Winston Churchill changed all that. His bulldog-like defiance of Adolf Hitler and his impassioned speeches rallying the British people struck a

CHURCHILL

Right: King George VI and Queen Elizabeth visiting British airborne troops in southern England, May 1944. Such visits by the King and Queen played an important role in helping to boost morale among the Allied fighting men.

Left: The friendly invasion! An English village Rector and his wife get to know two American officers, entertained to tea in the Rectory garden. Such hospitality was regularly extended by British families towards their American guests as the US presence in the United Kingdom swelled to more than a million.

Above: American troops undergoing assault training on Slapton Sands in Devon. Slapton Sands, lying between the villages of Strete and Torcross, was to be the scene of the tragic disaster of Operation TIGER in April 1944.

chord that transformed the spirit of the nation. With grim determination the British set about defending their island. During August and September 1940 the Royal Air Force (RAF) successfully defeated the German *Luftwaffe*'s massive air assault on southern England in what became known as the Battle of Britain. Angered by this setback and at the same time keenly aware that the Royal Navy still controlled the seas around the island, Hitler decided to postpone indefinitely his plans for invasion. Even the nightly bombing raids on London and other British cities, which continued throughout the winter and spring of 1940–41, failed to break the British spirit. Finally, in June 1941, Hitler turned his attention eastward and his armies marched instead on the Soviet Union. Against all the odds, therefore, Britain managed stubbornly to survive. Supported by the countries of the Commonwealth and Empire and with supplies and armaments flowing in

from a still unswervingly neutral United States, she remained a lone bastion of freedom on the edge of continental Europe.

By the Spring of 1944, however, the wheel had turned full circle. The island that had itself faced the threat of invasion four years earlier had become the springboard for the liberation of Western Europe. Throughout 1942 and 1943 supplies had poured across the Atlantic in a steady stream. Troops from the United States and Canada began to arrive in their thousands. Cheerful and confident, they filed down the gangways onto the quaysides of Belfast, Liverpool and the Clyde. Soon there were nearly 1.5 million American ground troops and another 500,000 airmen and sailors in the United Kingdom. They joined a rapidly growing British Army that had been training hard in preparation to invade the continent. In addition, there were thousands more men and women from the occupied countries of Europe who had managed to reach Britain to

THE AMERICANS ARRIVE

PREPARATIONS

carry on the fight. There were Free French, wearing the shoulder flash of the Cross of Lorraine, who had rallied to the leadership of General De Gaulle, as well as Poles, Czechs, Belgians, Dutch and Norwegians.

Britain, in fact, had been transformed into an armed camp. The signs of military preparedness were visible wherever one looked. The roads, largely denuded of civilian traffic as a result of tight fuel rationing, had been taken over by army lorries, jeeps and tracked vehicles. Columns of troops and tanks were everywhere on the move. In the fields and woods of southern England great

military camps had suddenly sprung up. Guns, engineering stores and ammunition dumps were concealed under camouflage netting. Massive vehicle parks appeared in which lines of new Sherman tanks were concentrated in an impressive display. Across the flat countryside of eastern England, from Yorkshire to the Thames, whole sections of agricultural land had been turned into new airfields. American aircraft began to appear in ever greater numbers: Mustang fighter planes, Dakota transports, Liberator bombers and the heavily armed Boeing Flying Fortresses. Soon the distinctive white star

Right: A scene that vividly illustrates what Britain was like in the spring of 1944. A housewife unconcernedly goes about the task of hanging out her washing in the garden while the street outside is jammed solid with guns and military vehicles.

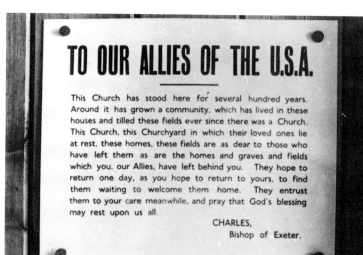

TO OUR ALLIES OF THE U.S.A.

This Church has stood here for several hundred years. Around it has grown a community, which has lived in these houses and tilled these fields ever since there was a Church. This Church, this Churchyard in which their loved ones lie at rest, these homes, these fields are as dear to those who have left them as are the homes and graves and fields which you, our Allies, have left behind you. They hope to return one day, as you hope to return to yours, to find them waiting to welcome them home. They entrust them to your care meanwhile, and pray that God's blessing may rest upon us all.

CHARLES,
Bishop of Exeter.

Above: As the people of south Devon hand over their homes and villages to provide a training ground for the US Army, the Church authorities offer a heartfelt prayer to the new occupants.

Right: American Boeing B 17F Flying Fortresses ready for take-off at an airfield in eastern England. During 1943–44 bombers of the RAF and USAAF carried out round-the-clock raids on German cities and towns.

emblem of the United States Army Air Force became as familiar to the British as the red, white and blue roundels of their own Royal Air Force. Night after night, day after day, bomber planes of both Allied air forces took off from their bases to attack targets deep inside Hitler's Reich. The roar of their engines filled the skies.

In the streets of London, badly scarred by German bombing, a colourful cosmopolitan presence brightened the grey drabness of wartime. The accents and uniforms of a score of nations proliferated. Americans in particular were everywhere. Genial gum-chewing GIs, out for a good time and with money to spend, virtually took over parts of London's fashionable West End, which echoed with the voices of Texas, Chicago and the Bronx. The famous Rainbow Corner Club in Piccadilly became the Mecca for all American servicemen who found themselves in Britain's capital city. The social impact of this American invasion on British families was immense. Friendly, uninhibited, easy-going, these young Americans quickly broke down the instinctive reserve of their British hosts, who marvelled at the relative wealth and material luxuries of their transatlantic allies. Many lasting friendships were made. For many British girls in particular the arrival of the

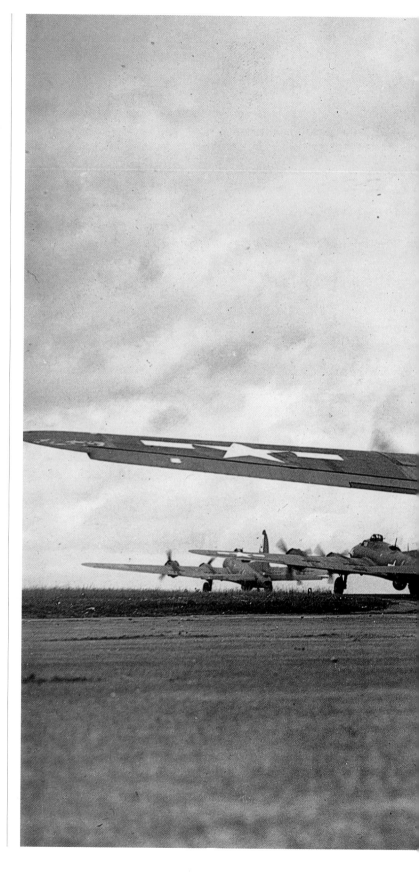

Americans came as the greatest thrill of their young lives.

Accommodating this vast assembly of troops and equipment landed the British with a major headache. It was not just a question of finding them billets and places where they could set up camp; it was necessary also to make available places where they could train. Most of the American soldiers had no combat experience, and it was vital that they should be able to carry out full-scale exercises – above all rehearsals of sea landings – if they were to be ready and fully prepared when the day of invasion came.

Geographical logic dictated their disposition. For the most part the American ground forces were assigned to the southwest peninsula of England, from where they were later destined to embark to form the western wing of the Allied invasion front. The lanes and villages of the counties of Somerset, Dorset, Devon and Cornwall were quickly turned into a mini-America. Young Americans thronged the village pubs, often outnumbering the local population who began to wonder what had hit them. The country around Slapton Sands in South Devon was designated a major training zone for the

DISPOSITION OF AMERICAN TROOPS

Below: The voice of Free France. General de Gaulle reviewing Free French naval commandos on parade in London during 1944.

Report by Guy Byam of the BBC who landed with the British Paratroops on D-Day morning

The rear gunner yelled suddenly, 'The glider's hit'. The skipper said, 'Glider pilot, glider pilot, are you alright?' There was a short pause and then the voice came again: 'Alright. We're with you'. The navigator all this time had been working with his maps and rulers. He was shouting to the skipper. And when we came out of the cloud and away from the flak, why, there was the landing zone just as we had studied it on maps for days and days. 'Casting off', said the little gruff voice. And we could just hear a faint 'Thanks, Skipper and good luck', as the tug lunged forward, free of the glider's weight. I looked down as we went into a turn to come home. There was nothing but blackness now, but there were a lot of gliders swishing down in that blackness.

United States Army, and many villagers and farmers were moved out of their homes, a sacrifice that did not go unrecognized by the Americans. Other American forces were stationed in South Wales. The beautiful Gower Peninsula near Swansea, whose beaches were thought to resemble some of the beaches on the Channel coast of France, was another area marked out for pre-invasion training.

The eastern half of Britain was the province of the British and Canadian forces. This was their training ground. East Anglia and the southeastern counties of Hampshire, Surrey, Sussex and Kent teemed with the berets and darker khaki serge of British uniforms – an army that had a long-standing score to settle with Hitler and who knew that the day of decision was at last drawing near.

CHAPTER FIVE

The Allied Plan

The question of who was to become Supreme Commander of the Allied liberation army that was gathering in Britain was finally decided in December 1943. It had been agreed that the appointment should be given to an American, as it was recognized that eventually the Americans would provide the major part of the Allied land forces in Europe. The choice fell upon a 54-year-old Texan-born general, Dwight D. Eisenhower, who at the time was the Allied Commander in North Africa. Eisenhower – or 'Ike' as both Americans and British called him – had until then been a relatively little-known figure. His military career had not been particularly distinguished. He had no first-hand experience of battle or of command in the field. Essentially, he was a back-room general, a committee man and a planner. And therein lay his strength. Eisenhower was a man of great personal charm, with a rare ability to get along with people. He was tactful, diplomatic, conciliatory but he also knew how to be tough when the occasion demanded. President Roosevelt picked Eisenhower for those very qualities, and it was an inspired choice. For Eisenhower's task was not only to plan and oversee a cross-Channel invasion, but also to smooth out differences between the Americans and British and ensure accord between the various commanders, some of whom could be notoriously difficult. It was a mark of Eisenhower's success that he very soon became extremely popular with the British.

The Deputy Supreme Commander was a Briton, Air Chief Marshal Sir Arthur Tedder. This senior RAF officer was a man of polish and high intelligence. Moreover, he knew Eisenhower well, having worked with him closely when he had commanded the Allied Air Forces in the Mediterranean theatre, and, fortunately, the two men held each other in mutual high regard.

The rest of the Allied Supreme Command team was confirmed in January 1944. Royal Navy Admiral Sir Bertram Ramsay was appointed Allied Naval Commander. An officer of great experience, Ramsay was the mastermind behind the successful evacuation of the British Army from Dunkirk in 1940. He had helped in the planning of the Allied landings in French North Africa in 1942 and had also commanded a naval task force during the invasion of Sicily. His attention to detail was a byword and he was an acknowledged master of logistical planning.

Air Chief Marshal Sir Trafford Leigh-Mallory was named Commander-in-Chief of the Allied Air Forces. He too was a formidable figure, who had commanded one of the two key RAF fighter groups in the Battle of Britain. No equivalent commander of Allied land forces was appointed, however. Instead General Sir Bernard Montgomery, the victor of El Alamein, was brought back to Britain from Italy to take command of all the Allied land forces in the assault stage of Operation OVERLORD. It was agreed that General Eisenhower would personally take over from him once the Supreme Commander had been able to establish his headquarters on French soil.

EISENHOWER

MONTGOMERY

Right: General Dwight D. Eisenhower, the Allied Supreme Commander, studying a wall map of the European theatre of operations. This picture was taken shortly before D-Day, 6 June.

Montgomery was in many ways an awkward man to get along with. His somewhat ascetic habits and overbearing self-confidence irritated even his closest colleagues, and his relations with the Americans were often far from cordial. But, for all his faults of personality, Montgomery was an experienced and highly competent general; a professional soldier with a shrewd grasp of military essentials, trusted implicitly by his men. Moreover, he and Rommel were old adversaries in the Western Desert and he had studied the German Field Marshal's tactics and the way his mind worked. There was no-one better qualified to lead the Allied assault on Hitler's fortress.

The two Americans on the Supreme Command were Lieutenant General Omar N. Bradley and Lieutenant General Walter Bedell Smith. Bradley was known as a tough no-nonsense officer who had been a friend of Eisenhower since their early days together in the Military Academy at West Point. Having been a corps commander in North Africa and in Sicily, he was promoted to take charge of the United States 1st Army in the planned invasion of Normandy. Bedell Smith, who had served with General Eisenhower in North Africa and in the Mediterranean, retained his special position as the Supreme Commander's Chief of Staff. Finally, Britain's General Morgan, who as COSSAC had played such an important role in the initial invasion planning, was appointed a Deputy Chief of Staff. Eisenhower spoke openly about the debt he owed to Morgan, while Morgan himself soon became one of the Supreme Commander's most fervent admirers. 'There was a man sent by God and his name was Ike', Morgan later remarked.

JANUARY 1944

Eisenhower set up his headquarters at Bushy Park near Kingston upon Thames, on the western outskirts of London, and at the end of January 1944 the Allied Command team got down to work. It did not take them long to realize that the original COSSAC plan to invade the French coast along a front of about 30 km (20 miles) was quite impracticable. Montgomery insisted that the frontage of the assault landing was too narrow to enable him to form a bridgehead large enough to accommodate the follow-up invasion force. It was agreed to increase the width of the landing area to almost 95 km (60 miles).

INVASION PLAN:
SEABORNE

The broad outline of the invasion plan was that the Allies would attack the Normandy coast at three locations:

1　The Americans would land on the southeast corner of the Cotentin Peninsula on the northwest side of the Vire Estuary. The stretch of beach targeted for the landing was given the code name UTAH.

2　A second American landing would be made on the eastern side of the Vire near the village of Vierville-sur-Mer on a beach given the code name OMAHA.

3　At the same time, about 16 km (10 miles) to the east of OMAHA, British and Canadian troops would be put ashore along a 39-km (24-mile) stretch of coast between the small port of Arromanches and the mouth of the River Orne, north of the city of Caen. The combined British and Canadian assault forces would be approximately equal in number to the Americans.

These seaborne landings would be preceded during the hours of darkness by an aerial invasion by three airborne divisions, two American and one British. The American airborne force would land well inland from UTAH beach to secure exit routes for the seaborne forces across land flooded by the Germans. The British airborne division would land north and northeast of Caen to capture the Orne River crossings and secure the eastern flank of the Allied bridgehead.

INVASION PLAN:
AIRBORNE

Montgomery's intention, which Eisenhower understood and approved, was that the British should capture and hold Caen, shielding the Americans from any counterattack by the feared German panzer divisions stationed north and west of Paris. The Americans would meanwhile expand to the west and northwest, cutting off the port of Cherbourg. The swift capture of Cherbourg at the northern tip of the Cotentin Peninsula was a vital part of the Allied design, although Bradley did not believe it could be taken inside a fortnight at the earliest. From the outset Montgomery saw that the key to the success of the invasion would be Caen. It had to be made into a bastion, the pivot on which the eventual Allied break-out from the bridgehead would depend.

Altogether the Allied commanders planned to put eight divisions ashore on the first day of the invasion. This was easier said than done.

Omaha Beach: On the spot report from NBC reporter Thomas Traynor, also broadcast on the BBC

There were more dead men along a narrow path which led up the palisade. The column had stopped moving and I began to step past men, following a captain. Suddenly a voice said, 'Watch yourself, fellow, that's a mine'. A soldier sprawled on the bank was speaking. He had one foot half blown off. He had stepped on a mine a short time earlier. Now, while he waited for litter bearers, he'd been warning other soldiers about other mines in the vicinity. I can stand the dead, but the wounded horrify me, and I only looked at him to thank him. He looked very tired but perfectly collected. 'What you need is the medics', I said. 'I'll try and get them for you when I go back down'. 'Yeah', he said, 'but how they gonna get up here?' He was right. The pathway was so clogged with men and so heavily mined that it was impassable. The engineers would have to get up here first.

SHORTAGE OF LANDING CRAFT

The complexities of the operation soon turned into an organizational nightmare. A main problem was an acute shortage of landing craft. These highly specialized craft were mostly American-built and came in a variety of shapes and sizes. The biggest was known as an LST, which stood for Landing Ship, Tanks, an ocean-going vessel that could carry up to 60 tanks or other vehicles and unload them through bow doors similar to a roll-on roll-off ferry. There were also smaller, flat-bottomed LCTs (Landing Craft, Tanks), which could hold four or five tanks and land them by running up onto the beach; LCIs (Landing Craft, Infantry), capable of carrying more than 200 troops; and the smaller LCAs (Landing Craft, Assault), which could be carried on board large ships and lowered into the sea by the davits. The Allies were hoping to land nearly 180,000 men and some 20,000 vehicles in Normandy on the first two days of the invasion. Without an adequate fleet of landing craft, especially the big tank-landing ships, there was little chance of achieving this aim. Churchill remarked in complete exasperation that 'the destinies of two great empires seem to be tied up in some goddamned things called LSTs!'

The problem was not so much a shortage of numbers of landing craft as the fact that they were all in the wrong place. Some were in the Pacific under the control of the US Navy, whose Commander-in-Chief, Admiral Ernest King, was reluctant to hand them over to the European theatre of operations. Others were in the Mediterranean, allocated for operations in Italy and for an eventual invasion of southern France. It took several months of bitter argument and haggling before the necessary craft were released so that Operation OVERLORD could go ahead.

Sea transport was not the only difficulty. The OVERLORD planners had been given control over the fighters and fighter bombers of the 2nd British Tactical Air Force (TAF) and the American 9th TAF, but they quickly realized that this would not be enough to ensure the success of the operation. What they needed was the massive air power of the RAF and USAAF Strategic Bomber Forces, which were commanded by Air Chief Marshal Sir Arthur Harris and General Carl Spaatz respectively. Neither Harris nor Spaatz was willing to give up control of the heavy bombers, which were fully engaged in attacking targets inside Germany. They did not object to supporting OVERLORD on the day of invasion, but they did not want to switch their bombers from Germany to soften up the German road and rail infrastructure in France in the weeks preceding the invasion. The issue developed into a blazing row between the OVERLORD Supreme Command and the bomber barons. Eisenhower finally managed to get his way, but not before he was on the point of threatening to resign.

Aside from these political disputes, there

QUARREL OVER AIR SUPPORT

Right: The Supreme Command Allied Expeditionary Force, February 1944. From left to right: Lieutenant General Omar N. Bradley, Admiral Sir Bertram H. Ramsay, Air Chief Marshal Sir Arthur Tedder, General Dwight D. Eisenhower, General Sir Bernard Montgomery, Air Chief Marshal Sir Trafford Leigh-Mallory and Lieutenant General Walter Bedell Smith.

were other major practical problems to overcome. First, there was the question of the tides. The initial idea had been to make the landings at high tide so that the landing craft could be carried close into the shore. The Allied discovery that Rommel was planting explosive devices below the high-water level necessitated a rapid change of plan. To come in at low tide would certainly allow the engineers and explosive experts to defuse and clear these beach obstacles, but it also meant that the assault troops would have a longer distance to wade ashore under enemy fire. In the end Montgomery decided to compromise.

He proposed that the landings be made at mid-tide to give the engineers time to clear paths through the obstacles so that the follow-up craft could get through. This required the most accurate and precise timing. The tides in the English Channel come in earlier in the west than in the east, as the currents move in a westerly flow from the Atlantic. This meant that the actual landing times on the various beaches would have to be staggered, with the Americans on UTAH beach going in first.

The investigation of the proposed landing beaches was carried out with the utmost care.

For months the British photographed the entire coast of northern France. RAF Spitfires flew at almost wave level in order to take pictures of the beaches as they would appear to the invading forces from the sea. Models were made of the countryside behind the beaches, indicating the main geographical features and landmarks. When the British learned in January 1944 that some of the beaches might contain soft peat and clay patches that could bog down Allied tanks they launched an extraordinary expedition. A British midget submarine carrying two military scientists sailed to the Normandy coast and lay submerged offshore while the scientists swam to the beach. The expedition was not only able to assure the Allied Command that the sands were firm, but it also managed to bring back valuable information about the structure of the beach and the nature of the German defences. British commando frogmen carried out similar reconnaissance forays, swimming to the shore under cover of darkness. Luckily none was ever spotted or captured. As a result of these surveys the Allies were able to build up a comprehensive picture of the targeted invasion coast well in advance. Millions of maps were printed covering the Normandy area in minute detail.

With an operation the magnitude and importance of OVERLORD, nothing could be left to chance. The lives of thousands of men depended on getting it right. Many ingenious ideas were put forward, two of which turned out to be of major significance. Having learned from the Dieppe experience that they could not count on capturing a port in which to land supplies, the Allies decided to take one with them. They would build an artificial port in England and later tow it across the Channel.

The second brainwave that was acted upon concerned fuel supplies. One of the great worries for the Allied planners was the risk involved in bringing in oil tankers, which would be vulnerable to air and submarine attack. They therefore proposed to lay an oil pipeline under the Channel to bring fuel direct from England to France. It was given the code name PLUTO, which stood, of course, for Pipe Line Under The Ocean.

CHAPTER SIX

Secrecy and Deception

D-DAY

The target date for the invasion was set for the first week in June. The invasion day itself was given the code name D-DAY, by which name it has passed into history. Originally it had been scheduled for early May, but it was put back a month largely because of the problem of assembling the necessary landing craft. However, the precise date for D-Day would not be decided until the last moment.

SECURITY

Far and away the most serious problem facing Eisenhower and his commanders was security. They were about to embark on the greatest amphibious military operation in the history of warfare, involving hundreds of thousands of men and huge flotillas of landing craft and ships. If successful, it could lead to a speedy end to the war in Europe. But if it failed, it would spell disaster, handing the initiative back to Hitler and reversing the entire course of the war. The Germans were naturally well aware that an invasion was being planned from Britain. What they did not know was where the attack would come, and when. They could make intelligent guesses but they did not know for certain. If the Germans were ever to find out, they could be ready and waiting and destroy the Anglo-American forces before they even got ashore.

FORTITUDE

To maintain the vital secrecy about the details of the invasion, the Allies devised an elaborate plan code-named FORTITUDE, to confuse and mislead the Germans. Its basic aim was to divert the attention of the Germans away from the Normandy coast and to persuade them that the attack would be launched against the Calais area, opposite the southeastern tip of England.

The great deception plan involved a wide variety of measures. Some were put into effect well in advance of the invasion; others were not set in train until D-Day itself. The first phase was to assemble what amounted to a phantom army in the region south and east of London. This fictitious force was given the title of United States First Army Group and its commander, for the purposes of deception only, was none other than General George S. Patton. Patton arrived in Britain early in 1944 to take command of the US 3rd army, which was building up in readiness to cross to France once the Spearhead forces had gained a substantial foothold. He was an aggressive general with a distinctly flamboyant style and had a fondness for sporting pearl handled Colt revolvers in his side holsters. The Germans knew all about him, since he had commanded the US forces that landed in Sicily the previous year. Therefore it was not hard to persuade them that Patton, who was a higher ranking general than Bradley, might actually be due to lead a cross-channel invasion. To reinforce the pretence of an American army waiting opposite Calais, Patton set up his headquarters not far from Dover and fake radio signals were sent out to give German radio monitors the impression of a large military set-up.

PATTON

In addition, scores of dummy landing craft were positioned in the River Thames, in the River Medway near Chatham and in a number of harbours in southeastern England.

Above: Dummy tank landing craft (LCTs) of rigid construction moored in a harbour on the southeastern coast of England as a decoy during preparations for the invasion of France.

At the same time hundreds of dummy tanks (many of them inflatable rubber balloons) were deployed conspicuously in the fields of Kent and Sussex, where they could be seen and photographed by German reconnaissance planes. This deception was kept up through to the day of invasion and beyond. In May, when the Allied Supreme Command had transferred its headquarters from London to Portsmouth, radio signals were first sent by landline to Dover and then transmitted, thereby giving the Germans the confirmation they needed that Montgomery's headquarters were also in southeast England. As a

piece of strategic duping it was masterly; the Germans were completely taken in.

The objective of wrong-footing the Germans was pursued by other even more subtle means, including air strikes. In the spring of 1944 the Allies carefully directed their massive bombing raids on northern France, mainly against targets east and north of the River Seine. Their aim was twofold: to cripple the French railway system so that reinforcements and supplies could not easily be moved to the Normandy region, and, by concentrating on the northeast region of France, harden the German belief that the

SPRING 1944

Pas-de-Calais was the invasion target. The Allies hoped that even when the attack on Normandy was launched the Germans would consider it only a feint and keep their reserves in position around Calais in readiness for the main assault.

SCOTTISH BLUFF

And this was not all. The FORTITUDE plan also involved the creation of yet another fictitious army, or rather two armies, in Scotland: a so-called British 4th Army and an equally bogus American 14th Army. A British officer, Colonel R.M. MacLeod, was ordered to Edinburgh to fashion this additional piece of bluff. Again the method was wireless traffic. A group of about 350 men and women set up in business fabricating a complex pattern of signals, following recognized British and American radio procedures. Messages went from army HQ through corps and division down to regiment. The two armies were even allotted their own nonexistent tactical air force. All in all, this ploy was designed to make the Germans believe that a force in excess of a quarter of a million men, including armoured divisions, was based in Scotland. Their target? It could only be Norway.

SCANDINAVIA:
AN ALLIED DECOY

The Germans were, of course, not fooled into supposing that the main thrust of an Allied invasion would be made against Scandinavia, but the threat of an attack across the North Sea was enough to make sure that Hitler would not remove any of his 17 divisions in Norway and Denmark to strengthen his forces in northern France. During 1942 and 1943, the British had carried out a number of highly successful commando raids on the Norwegian coast, emphasizing their ability to inflict damaging strikes against this northernmost sector of the Atlantic Wall. These raids were continued in 1944, resulting in the destruction of coastal shipping and the blowing up of an oil refinery. At the same time American aircraft carried out photographic reconnaissance missions along the coasts of Norway and Sweden. The Russians,

too, entered into the spirit of things, deliberately leaking false information about a projected landing on the coast of the Barents Sea in northern Finland.

Hitler was highly sensitive to the threat of an Allied attack upon Scandinavia. Norway not only protected Germany's northern flank, but also provided vital bases for its U-Boats and for the *Luftwaffe*, while Sweden, though officially a neutral country, supplied ball bearings and the iron ore upon which the German armaments industry relied. Knowing Hitler's concern, the Allies maintained the deception, even to the extent of placing orders for thousands of skis. Similar false reports spread by Allied agents in Sweden helped to arouse German suspicions that a joint British-American/Soviet operation in the north of Europe was only weeks away. Perhaps the nicest touch of all was BBC radio in Scotland broadcasting a performance by the 'Pipe Band of the 4th Army' beating retreat at Edinburgh Castle!

RADAR

The other key element in the deception was timed to coincide with the invasion assault. Allied Intelligence had established that the entire Normandy coastline was crammed full

Above: Another clever piece of Allied deception. A dummy Sherman tank, one of hundreds deployed in southeast England to suggest an army in waiting opposite Calais. The dummy could be blown up like a barrage balloon and, when deflated, would pack into a small suitcase!

with German radar, which would be able to detect an invasion fleet assembling long before it sailed from the British coast. Somehow that radar had to be rendered ineffective.

The answer was an ingenious combination of radar jamming and electronic trickery. The Allies installed powerful jamming equipment in both ships and aircraft to blot out German long-range detection from the radar stations situated between Cherbourg and Le Havre. At the same time they planned to send a decoy force of small ships towards Boulogne and Calais just before the main invasion fleet set out for Normandy, thereby focusing German attention upon the Pas-de-Calais.

The decoy plan was nothing short of brilliant. Royal Navy motor launches would tow pieces of bent metal foil set under barrage balloons, which would give the impression on German radar screens of a fleet of big ships approaching. Meanwhile RAF bombers would fly overhead dropping bundles of foil

JAMMING AND TRICKERY

DECOY FORCE

The British Liberate Bayeux; BBC news bulletin, 8 June 1944

The first infantry and tanks moved in along the main road, and already French tricolours and Union Jacks were flying from rooftops and balconies. All our vehicles were brought to a dead stop by crowds of old men, women and children packing the main street. The whole town was hysterical with excitement and joy, and many of the old people simply stood there and cried. But all around there was a roar of cheering and shouting and waving; our troops were embraced, kissed, showered with roses and carnations, bottles of wine and glasses brought out and toasts drunk in the streets. The children were clambering over the jeeps and asking for souvenirs. Odd pennies and sixpences were produced and handed round. Then gradually the crowds split up and groups of our men were taken off to cafes and hotels and the celebration started all over again with much piano playing and singing of *God Save The King* and the *Marseillaise*.

Left: A dummy 25 pounder gun and trailer. Like the dummy LCTs, this was of rigid construction and could be collapsed and folded flat for storing.

strips, which would appear as landing craft moving behind the bigger vessels. The bombers would fly in continuous circles, moving steadily nearer the French coast and so producing the illusion of an invasion fleet heading straight for Calais.

PANICS AND ALARMS

In spite of all their stringent security measures and deception ploys the Allied commanders lived in constant fear that the secret of the time and place of the invasion would leak out. During the immediate run up to D-Day they went through some nightmare moments. By far the most serious incident was a disaster that took place barely six weeks before the invasion was due. At the end of April 1944 three US divisions together with naval and air units were scheduled to take part in a major training exercise code-named Operation TIGER. It was, in fact, designed as a rehearsal for the forthcoming landing on UTAH beach in Normandy, only this time Normandy would be the South Devon coast and the exercise would be watched by Eisenhower, Bradley and other Supreme Allied Commanders. Operation TIGER began on 27 April and the American troops duly went ashore from their landing craft at Slapton Sands south of Dartmouth. However, the operation provided for a follow-up convoy of big landing craft which was to arrive the next morning. And this was when disaster struck.

Early on 28 April, during the hours of darkness, a slow moving convoy of eight heavily loaded LSTs escorted by a single British corvette was making its way across Lyme Bay towards the South Devon coast when it was attacked by a flotilla of German E-Boats. The Germans had picked up the movement of the convoy on their radar screens and the naval base at Cherbourg was alerted. E-Boats, or *Schnellboote* as the Germans rightly called them, were long, slim,

exceptionally fast patrol boats armed with four torpedoes and a 40-mm gun. The British, who knew only too well the menace these patrol craft represented to Allied shipping in the English Channel, had in fact sent some of their own motor torpedo boats and four destroyers to keep watch on the French coast directly opposite the area of the American manoeuvres. But the E-Boats, keeping radio silence and with their radar switched off, managed to slip through the British naval screen. Moving at high speed, they hit the convoy without warning. Flitting around the landing craft like grey shadows, they loosed off a volley of torpedoes before the Americans and British knew what was happening. Within seconds they had torpedoed and sunk two of the LSTs and damaged two others. The death toll was catastrophic. Around 750 Americans were killed or missing, most of them troops belonging to the US 1st Engineer Special Brigade.

As the bodies of the victims were washed ashore after dawn and the full scale of the disaster became known, the Allied Commanders were in turmoil. They dare not let the news get out. Eisenhower ordered that complete secrecy should be observed and the dead were temporarily buried in a mass grave within the exercise area. It was not only the heavy loss of life that concerned Eisenhower and his staff. A number of the American officers who were missing had been given the top security classification BIGOT. That meant that they were privy to some of the details of the coming invasion. The fear was that they might have been picked out of the water by the E-Boats and taken back to France for interrogation. But after thorough investigation Allied security pronounced itself satisfied that no prisoners had been taken. Eisenhower and Montgomery were assured that the Normandy invasion could go ahead as it had been planned.

Nonetheless, the Lyme Bay tragedy

Right: Vehicles, guns and ammunition were stored under camouflage netting throughout the fields and woods of southern England. Britain was soon turned into a gigantic armed camp.

sister in Chicago beneath the correct military address and the packet had accordingly been put into the US domestic mail.

In another scare during the May, copies of the outline plan for OVERLORD were blown by a gust of wind out of a window of the War Office in London. Staff rushed out into Whitehall, scrabbling furiously to pick them up as they scattered across the street. Fortunately all the papers were recovered.

But easily the most bizarre and seemingly inexplicable incident was that of the crossword puzzle of the British newspaper, the *Daily Telegraph*. At the beginning of May the crossword contained a clue asking for the name of one of the American states. The answer was UTAH. Later in the month came a clue relating to a tribe of Indians on the Missouri. The answer was OMAHA. As if this was not enough to set alarm bells ringing, there followed in rapid succession further clues to which the answers were OVERLORD, MULBERRY and NEPTUNE. The last two words happened to be the code names of the secret prefabricated port under construction on the Thames and of the naval operation designed to carry the invasion army to Normandy. The coincidence was just too great and MI5 at once began an inquiry. The two innocent schoolmasters who had compiled the *Daily Telegraph*'s crossword were interrogated and eventually cleared. They knew nothing of the D-Day planning and their choice of clues was just one of those incredible million-to-one chances, although doubts lingered in some sections of British Intelligence for a considerable time after these remarkable events.

remained a closely guarded secret for nearly forty years after the war was over. But this was not the only fright the Allies had. In one case a packet containing top-secret BIGOT classification documents was sent in error to a private address in Chicago, an area of the city, incidentally, where there was a large German American community. The packet burst open during sorting in the Chicago post office, where the staff became suspicious about the contents and called in the FBI. An investigation soon revealed that an American army dispatch clerk in London had absent-mindedly scribbled down the address of his

CHAPTER SEVEN

Hobart's Funnies

The problem of how to overcome the German beach defences had been worrying the British ever since the Dieppe raid of 1942. And in March 1943 the Chief of the Imperial General Staff, Sir Alan Brooke, ordered the setting up of an experimental unit to see if technology could provide some answers. This unit was the 79th Armoured Division and its commander was an acknowledged specialist in tank warfare, Major General Percy Hobart.

Hobart and his engineers duly set to work and by May 1944 they had come up with an extraordinary range of armoured vehicles that no other army in the world possessed. The first and potentially most valuable invention was an amphibious tank. Hobart took a standard American Sherman and fitted it with twin propellers that could be driven by the tank's main engine, and placed a waterproof canvas skirt around its body, leaving the caterpillar tracks exposed. The tank could be launched into the sea several miles offshore and driven straight up onto the beach, where the skirt would be collapsed and the gun turret be ready for action. Known as Duplex Drive (DD) tanks, these ingenious vehicles were to prove one of the great surprises of the D-Day landings.

In addition to the DD tank, Hobart created a special Crab 'Flail' tank, which had whirling chain flails that could smash a path through enemy minefields, exploding the mines as it went along. To deal with the problem of soft sand Hobart and his team of engineers produced the Bobbin tank. Again,

this was essentially a standard tank, this time fitted with a steel superstructure upon which a giant bobbin or cotton reel was mounted. The Bobbin lumbered forward, laying as it went a canvas roadway, which provided a stable base for other vehicles over treacherous areas of beach.

To knock out the strongly built German pillboxes Hobart adapted a heavily armoured British Churchill Mark III tank, installing a short-range 25-lb mortar as well as a machine gun. The explosive power of the mortar at point-blank range was devastating. It was to

DD TANKS

CRAB 'FLAIL' TANKS

BOBBIN TANKS

Right: British Duplex Drive (DD) amphibious tanks being checked out at Gosport near Portsmouth early in 1944. The picture shows the tanks with their canvas screens deflated. The DD tanks were to be used on both the British and American beaches on D-Day.

Left: One of the ingenious 'Bobbin' tanks designed by Major General Hobart of the British 79th Armoured Division. Picture taken in April 1944. This was a British Churchill Mark III tank designed to lay a canvas carpet across treacherous soft sand on the beaches. Each carpet extended more than 100 m (320 ft).

prove a deadly weapon. Another intended shock to the Germans was the so-called 'Crocodile'. This ugly-looking vehicle was a Churchill tank with a high-pressure flame-thrower that could shoot a jet of flame up to 90m (300ft), effectively incinerating everything in its path.

Finally, there was the Churchill Mark III AVRE vehicle, which resembled a mobile crane more than a tank. In front was a long boom or derrick that could lay sections of steel girder bridges over ditches, small rivers and causeways. It carried a crew of five and was armed with a powerful mortar and a machine gun.

Hobart's specialized armour – or 'funnies'

Left: A 'Crab' flail tank in action. This converted Sherman M4 tank proved one of the most useful of Hobart's box of tricks. Its whirling chain flails could clear a path 3.5 m (11 ft) wide through enemy minefields.

Hobart's box of tricks were for some reason never accepted by the Americans – a mistake that would sadly cost them dear when the day of invasion came.

Above: The mastermind behind the 'Funnies': Major General Sir Percy Hobart explaining a point to General Sir Miles Dempsey, Commander of the British 2nd Army, during a rehearsal of Hobart's new equipment.

as they came to be known – were classic examples of British wartime inventiveness at its best. They were to make a significant contribution to the eventual success of the D-Day landings, especially on the British-targeted beaches. Montgomery was enthusiastic about them the first moment he saw them being demonstrated and adapted his battle plan to make the maximum use of their highly specific features.

Unfortunately, although the British offered their 'funnies' to the Americans, Eisenhower and Bradley showed interest only in the swimming DD tanks, of which a number were ordered. The Crab 'Flail' tanks, the flame-throwing 'Crocodiles' and the rest of

Frank Gillard of the BBC recorded on the control ship off the French coast on D-Day morning, 6 June 1944, watching the assault craft get under way

Up on the tiny flag deck a senior naval officer stands beside the Skipper, a microphone in his hand. Behind him is the trumpet of his loud-hailer. By swinging it in the right direction he can make himself heard across hundreds of yards of water. It's coming up to time. Not zero hour yet, but zero hour minus. The moment when the assault craft are to set off from their assembly area for the beaches. The convoy has come to a standstill. Engines are ticking over. The mother ships – the troopships – have been lowering their assault craft into the water. A minesweeper comes sliding alongside us out of the blackness. A voice calls from her, thin and strained. Our loud-hailer comes aloud with a click. 'Hello there', it says, 'Glad to see you. Everything alright? What do you make of our exact position? . . . Good, that checks with our own calculations. We're OK thanks.' And off goes the shape into the darkness.

Astern of us the assault craft are now assembled. You know that they are neatly marshalled there in formation, but you can only make out the leaders. The loud hailer checks them over. Voices reply faintly out of the darkness. The naval commander is looking at his watch. He puts the microphone to his mouth. 'Off you go, then, and good luck to you.' Engines rev up and those small dark shapes come abreast of you, row after row of them, and shoot ahead like so many dark beetles on the surface of the water. You feel you want to give them a cheer as they pass.

CHAPTER EIGHT

OVERLORD – The Spring is Coiled

Left: A column of American troops on the march to an embarkation port in southern England.

SECURITY MEASURES

By the middle of May 1944 final rehearsal exercises for the invasion of Normandy had been completed and the plan for OVERLORD began to move into top gear. General Eisenhower had set the provisional date for D-Day as Monday, 5 June and all the spearhead forces had to be at the ports and ready for embarkation by 1 June. Strict security measures had already been imposed. During April the British government had declared that a 16-km (10-mile) belt around the southern and eastern coast of England and another along the Forth estuary in Scotland were to be closed to all unauthorized visitors,

an order enforced by the police and military. At the same time movement of foreign diplomats was severely restricted and all civilian traffic between the United Kingdom and neutral Eire (Irish Republic) was stopped. The German and Japanese embassies in Dublin had become key espionage centres for relaying information coming out of Britain. At a stroke this important source of intelligence for the enemy was closed down.

The vast invasion army was at last on the move. Thousands of American, British and Canadian troops left their camps and training areas and headed for the coast. Convoys of

ON THE MOVE

Right: US medical
teams and stretcher
bearers boarding a
landing craft ready
for the cross-Channel
assault on Nazi-
occupied Europe.

Above: Hundreds of Sherman tanks lined up at an ordnance depot in Britain in readiness for shipment across the English Channel. The Sherman was the standard Allied tank used in the Normandy invasion, but the more heavily armoured British Churchill Mark III as well as light-medium Cromwell and Valentine tanks also took part.

Robert Dunnet of the BBC with American troops at an embarkation port, broadcoast on 6 June 1944

I lived with American troops in the barracks where they passed their enforced 'purdah' (confinement). And all day long the huge concrete squares rang with the sound of their energy. They played interminable games of volleyball and football and baseball. Then suddenly one morning the squares, instead of being full of racing figures, were dotted with heaps of equipment in long lines. The men stood by their individual piles with their helmets and rifles and life belts around their waists. They piled into lorries and saw the leafy English countryside rush away. And they waved and whistled at the girls. They came by main roads and by lanes, by night and by day, and all their journeys led to one or other of the many points by the sea. The men stood in their lines by the shore, waiting for the boats that were to take them out to the bigger ships. And they saw for the first time something of the size of the operation – although everyone saw only one little bit. At our point of embarkation before the assault, they counted the Tank Landing Ships here and the Infantry Landing Craft there and watched dozens of Infantry Assault Craft dashing about among the bigger ships carrying the troops from the shore. They were quiet in the main, although there were always one or two to wave and whistle to the seagoing British WRENS on some of the little ferry boats.

armoured vehicles and trucks passed at night through the blacked-out sleeping towns and villages to converge on the embarkation ports of southern England, from Falmouth in the west to Ipswich in the east. Columns of marching troops in full battle order moved into the sealed assembly compounds to await the summons to board their transport ships. English villagers who had for so many months been used to the presence of soilders from the camp down the road awoke one morning to find them gone. Most of Britain sensed that the long-awaited invasion was now imminent, but miraculously the word never got out. Allied security was tight and the secret kept.

Allied Intelligence, however, was never sure how much the Germans knew. Early in May the Allied commanders were shocked to discover that German forces in the Normandy region were being rearranged and strengthened. The 21st Panzer Division was moved from Brittany to a position just south of Caen, ominously close to the designated British landing area. Another crack division, Panzer Lehr, was moved close to Le Mans, scarcely a day's drive from Caen, and an infantry division and a parachute regiment were transferred to the southern part of the Cotentin Peninsula in the very area where the two US airborne divisions were due to drop.

The Allied Supreme Commanders were thoroughly alarmed. Everything pointed to the Germans having learned of the Allies' invasion plan. In fact, the German reinforcement of the Normandy region was due entirely to a hunch on the part of Hitler himself. Hitler, it was discovered later, had a growing belief that Normandy would, after all, be the Allied target. Fortunately for the British and Americans, Hitler's uncanny intuition never communicated itself to the German generals. Von Rundstedt and the German High Command in the west never wavered in their conviction that the real

GERMAN MOVEMENTS

HITLER'S HUNCH

invasion attempt would be launched against the Pas-de-Calais, so the powerful 15th Army, guarding the coast between Le Havre and Ostend, remained in place.

The last weeks of May were a time of tension and uncertainty for all the Allied troops waiting in Britain. The senior commanders realized the need to calm fears and engender a spirit of confidence among their men. No-one was more assiduous in this task than Montgomery. Standing on a small platform, he would gather the troops around him and address them on the task before them. British and Americans alike gave a rapturous welcome to this slight figure wearing a black beret, who talked to them in language they could understand. Speaking in clipped tones, he radiated an aura of confidence that at once transmitted itself to his listeners. Montgomery was particularly good with American troops, who, unlike some American generals, came to revere him. Visits by King George VI, Eisenhower, Bradley and Sir Miles Dempsey (Commander of the British 2nd Army) also played an important role in boosting morale.

Once in the assembly areas, the troops were not allowed out. This was the hardest time for the men of the eight divisions who were to lead the invasion, the spearhead troops. Crammed into their confined quarters, there was little for them to do but master their impatience and wait. All were aware that before long they would be going to what many of them termed 'the far shore', but exactly where and when they did not know.

The first inkling of what was to happen came in the last week of May, when the troops were issued with French francs, sea-sickness pills and, in the case of the British, a booklet which told them in plain terms that they were going to assist in the task of 'pushing the Germans out of France and back where they belong'. After that the secret was

MONTGOMERY

Left: General Sir Bernard Montgomery, C-in-C Allied land forces for the invasion, addressing troops of the Royal Ulster Rifles, May 1944. Montgomery gave many such informal talks in the run-up to D-Day, visiting troops of all the Allied armies.

Right: And still they come! The build up of the Allied armies in Britain in the months before D-Day. Here, Canadian troops are seen disembarking at a British port after the voyage across the Atlantic.

TROOP BRIEFINGS

AIR FORCE BRIEFINGS

out. Inside the briefing huts the advance troops were given instructions on the job they were to do. The briefings were thorough down to the last detail. Each unit was taken step by step through the procedure it would go through on D-Day. Every move, every target was explained and illustrated. Models and photographs pinpointed the landing beaches, the obstacles, the minefields, the German gun emplacements and machine-gun nests. The troops were told who would deal with what, including the role to be played by the navy and the air force.

At air bases inland the glider pilots and crews of the airborne divisions were given similar close briefing of their target dropping zones. By the clever use of RAF film the pilots were able to see exactly what landmarks to look for to ensure that they landed the airborne divisions in the right areas.

Finally, at the beginning of June, the 150,000 men of the assault divisions moved out of their claustrophobic staging areas and down to the docks to board the waiting ships and landing craft. From Cornwall to the Thames Estuary British people living in the coastal towns watched with excitement as the embarkation took place. Lorries rumbled through the narrow streets of Fowey, Brixham, Weymouth, Poole, Shoreham and other south-coast harbours, ferrying troops and equipment. The invasion army was on board and waiting to go – what Eisenhower was later to describe as a great human spring coiled for the moment when it would vault the English Channel to the coast of France.

Left: OVERLORD gets under way. US troops loading trucks and equipment onto transport ships at an English south-coast harbour.

CHAPTER NINE

To Go or Not To Go

THE WEATHER

At the very last moment, with the invasion fleet poised to sail, fate in the shape of the weather intervened. This was the one factor over which the Allied commanders had no control, and it was crucial. Without the right weather conditions the whole invasion operation would be in serious jeopardy. It was essential that D-Day should have calm weather with little or no wind to whip up the sea in the Channel. Visibility had to be good enough for the Allied air forces to operate in support of the landings and there had to be enough moonlight for the airborne forces to see their dropping zones. The combination of moon and tides had to meet pre-set conditions and 5, 6 and 7 June were the only days that month which satisfied the necessary requirements.

All through May the weather in the English Channel area had been near perfect. There had been a succession of warm sunny days with cloudless skies and calm seas. But as May turned into June the weather underwent a sharp change. On Sunday, 4 June, the day before the invasion was due, Eisenhower and his commanders, meeting at Southwick House in Portsmouth, were told that the weather forecast for the following day was high winds, low cloud and fog. Eisenhower had no alternative but to postpone the invasion for 24 hours.

A TERRIBLE DILEMMA

The worsening weather situation faced the Allied chiefs with a terrible dilemma. Some ships of the invasion fleet had already put to sea and it was necessary to order them back to port to refuel and await orders to sail the

following day. But it was clear to all that the massive enterprise could not be postponed indefinitely. There was a limit to the length of time the fighting troops, keyed up for action, could be kept cooped up in their landing craft. Any further delay and they would lose the momentum and high morale that were so vital for success. Many American troops had

put to sea as early as 1 June in order to sail eastwards up the Channel to the naval rendezvous point and some of them were suffering the discomfort of seasickness as their ships pitched and tossed in the rising storm. For thousands of men, whether at sea or still at anchor in port, the strain of waiting was becoming unbearable.

Left: Waiting for D-Day. Hundreds of landing craft massed by the quayside in Southampton harbour in readiness for the invasion of Europe.

Lieutenant Commander George Honour DSC RNVR

Our task in X23 was to cross the Channel unobserved and set up a telescopic mast some 18 feet high with the beam pointing out to sea, which would act as a navigational beacon for the DD tanks which would be launched all around us. The mission was called Operation GAMBIT.

We left Gosport on the night of Friday, June 2nd 1944, and spent all Saturday and the following night crossing the Channel. On Sunday morning we reached the French coast and to our joy found that we were very close to our marking position. We observed the coast through our periscope and found it easy to fix our position as we had RAF photographs showing the churches and other landmarks on shore. There was even a light at the mouth of the River Orne. Having fixed our position, we bottomed and waited until nightfall. That night – the Sunday – we received a message that the invasion was being postponed. We didn't know for how long. So all we could do was to dive again to the seabed and wait for the Monday night. Surfacing again, we got a message that the invasion was on. This surprised us as the weather was as bad as the previous night. But anyway, we were very relieved as we had no idea how much oxygen we had left and were afraid it might run out before the invasion came. On the morning of June 6th at 0500 we surfaced, set up our lamp and beacons and waited for the invasion. As we came up through the hatch and looked seaward, there was nothing but ships – a great fleet from tiny landing craft to great battleships – stretching as far as the eye could see. By then the Allied bombardment had started and the shells were flying overhead, trying to winkle out the batteries on the shore . . .

We were especially relieved to get back to England safely, as, on looking up the word GAMBIT in a dictionary, we saw it was defined as 'the pawn you throw away in a game of chess'!

Eye witness account, dictated to author November 1992

4 JUNE

During the late evening of 4 June the Allied commanders gathered in the library of Eisenhower's headquarters at Southwick House to hear the latest forecast from the weather experts. The atmosphere was one of gloom and despondency. The rain beat against the windows and black storm clouds raced across the sky. The weather had turned with a vengeance and there seemed little chance that the invasion, so carefully planned, could now go ahead. But, to the commanders' surprise, the forecast contained a ray of hope. The senior meteorologist, Group Captain J.M. Stagg of the RAF, informed them that a break in the weather pattern was imminent. A short period of fair weather would begin the following day and last probably until the afternoon of Tuesday, 6 June. After that there would be three days of unsettled conditions, with some fair periods and variable cloud.

A RAY OF HOPE

The Allied commanders withdrew to consider in private the news given to them. The Supreme Commander asked his colleagues in turn what they felt they should now do. Should they take a gamble on the weathermen being right? Dare they grasp the slim chance that Group Captain Stagg had offered them and order the invasion on again? The two British Air Marshals, Tedder and Leigh-Mallory, were not optimistic, worried about the effect that the poor cloud conditions forecast for later in the week might have on bombing operations. However, Bedell Smith, Ramsay and Montgomery were inclined to take a chance. 'We've gotten a break we could hardly hope for' was the US general's comment. Eisenhower turned to Montgomery. 'Do you see any reason for not going on Tuesday?' Ike asked him. 'I would say – go', was Montgomery's reply.

The final decision lay with Eisenhower. He alone bore the awesome responsibility for deciding whether or not the whole gigantic enterprise should go ahead as planned, and the burden of eventual failure or success lay

EISENHOWER

Right: France, here we come! Cheerful British soldiers of the Royal Electrical and Mechanical Engineers reading the information booklet issued to them shortly before embarking for Normandy.

squarely upon his shoulders. For a few hushed moments Eisenhower reflected. Then he gave his historic verdict. 'Well, boys,' he said, 'I'm quite positive we must give the order. I don't like it, but there it is. I don't see how we can possibly do anything else.' Afterwards Eisenhower told Stagg, 'We've put it on again. For heaven's sake hold the weather to what you've forecast. Don't bring us any more bad news.'

At around dawn on the morning of Monday, 5 June, after a further consultation with the meteorologist, the commanders held one final meeting to confirm the decision. The weather report for 6 June was still favourable, although it was clear that the seas in the Channel would be choppy. By now optimism among the group had taken over and even Leigh-Mallory agreed that the chance had to be taken. Eisenhower closed the discussion, and the greatest amphibious operation in world history was ushered in with the almost casual words, 'OK. We'll go.' After the decision was taken, the Supreme Commander retired to his quarters to rest and read one of his favourite Westerns.

5 JUNE

'OK. WE'LL GO'

CHAPTER TEN

The Invasion Fleet

Right: Part of the huge Allied invasion fleet as it moves steadily towards the French coast in the grey light of dawn on 6 June 1944. The barrage balloons were designed to protect landing craft.

W ithin hours of the signal from Supreme Allied Headquarters the convoys of the invasion fleet once more put out to sea. As it happened, one convoy, which had sailed a few days earlier, had failed to receive Eisenhower's previous recall order. The convoy, carrying troops of the American 4th Infantry Division, was only turned back at the last moment, when it was almost in sight of the French coast. Fortunately, poor visibility prevented the Germans from spotting it.

Throughout Monday, 5 June, lines of ships and landing craft buffeted their way up the English Channel through a rough sea, with the wind blowing in savage gusts. American convoys from the ports of Falmouth, Plymouth, Torbay, Weymouth and Poole moved steadily eastwards to meet the British convoys pouring out from Southampton, Portsmouth, Shoreham, Newhaven, the Thames Estuary and Harwich. By evening they began to gather into a mighty fleet, the like of which the world had never seen. Their assembly point lay a short distance southeast of the Isle of Wight. Although officially known as Area Z, it quickly became known to the Royal Navy as 'Piccadilly Circus'.

A CLOSE SHAVE

THE FLEET ASSEMBLES

Right: A group of 'G.I. Joes' crammed on the deck of a landing craft of the US Coast Guard on the way to the Normandy beaches. Note the line of tethered barrage balloons, intended to ward off low-flying enemy aircraft.

ASSAULT FORMATION

Here the invasion force began to arrange itself into its assault formations. It divided into two main groups: the Eastern Task Force, commanded by Rear Admiral Sir Philip Vian of the Royal Navy, carrying the assault troops for the British beaches, and the Western Task Force, directed by Rear Admiral Alan C. Kirk of the US Navy, which would head for the American beaches of UTAH and OMAHA.

Altogether the fleet numbered more than 6,500 vessels, of which almost four-fifths were British and Canadian. Of the remainder, the bulk was American with a sprinkling of French, Dutch, Greek, Norwegian and Polish ships. The force comprised about 1,000

I do not recall any mention of fear on the way to France, although many like me must have felt a little worried at what the next 24 hours would hold in store. There was plenty of apprehension and some tension amongst the crew, but most of all there was an overriding excitement and pride that we were playing a leading role in the greatest sea-borne invasion the world had ever known. We all wondered how long it would take the Germans to spot us and how well we would be able to defend the armada against mass dive-bomber attacks.

Before passing through the minefield we became aware of a heavy drone above us that distracted us from the awesome spell of mine spotting. There was an endless line of shadows in the sky, which we realized to be a strong airborne force of men in gliders and 'tugs' or tow planes. In the half moonlight of that summer night we imagined – or did we really see – the force that was destined to make the first assault on the British sectors of the Normandy coast.

At 5.30am we closed to some two miles from the coast off Ouistreham and took up our bombarding position. As the light of dawn increased, the enormity of the invasion fleet became more apparent – the vast number of ships and craft of every description becoming visible, stretching as far as the eye could see. It was quite unbelievable. Someone said: 'What will the Germans on shore think when they see this lot?'

Petty Officer James R.B. Hinton, Royal Navy, who was aboard HMS *Scourge*, part of the 23rd Destroyer Flotilla that led the invasion fleet.

warships, including 7 battleships. The rest was made up of 4,000 landing craft and landing ships of various types, 730 ancillary ships and about 860 merchant vessels. Shortly before midnight this colossal armada began to move slowly southwards under cover of darkness. As the night wore on and D-Day, 6 June, dawned, the fleet bore down like grey

6 JUNE

ghosts on the coast of Normandy, 128 km (80 miles) to the south.

THE GREAT CRUSADE

Before leaving England the soldiers and sailors of the invasion force had received a personal message from General Eisenhower.

Left: D-Day, the naval bombardment. The 15-inch guns of the battleship HMS *Warspite* open up on enemy shore batteries at dawn on 6 June.

Right: X 23, Lieutenant George Honour's 17 m (57 ft)-long midget submarine, seen in choppy water off the French coast on D-Day at the end of her 72-hour mission to mark the British landing beaches.

Right: Sea rescue on D-Day. Survivors of a vessel sunk by a German mine are pulled from the water by the crew of a US Coast Guard landing barge. Many of the survivors were unconscious, being held afloat by their kapok life jackets.

MINESWEEPERS

FORTITUDE

THE MIDGET SUBS

They were, he told them, about to embark on a great crusade and the hopes and prayers of liberty-loving people everywhere marched with them. 'I have full confidence in your courage, devotion to duty and skill in battle', said the Supreme Commander. 'We will accept nothing less than full victory!'

The sailing of the fleet had been preceded by the dispatch of several flotillas of minesweepers, which carried out the urgent task of establishing mine-free lanes across the Channel. Some ten lanes were eventually cleared through which the invasion force was able to pass safely. The armada ploughed ahead in the form of an ungainly arc 80 km (50 miles) across. Around it the naval escorts bustled up and down, keeping watch for German E-boats and submarines, while overhead squadron after squadron of Allied fighters provided a powerful covering screen. As the invasion fleet made its way slowly across the Channel, the Allied deception plan – FORTITUDE – swung into action. German radar stations along the Normandy coast between Le Havre and Cherbourg were subjected to intensive jamming. At the same time the Royal Navy's operation to fool the Germans that an invasion force was approaching Calais rather than Normandy got under way assisted by the RAF. All that the German radar operators were allowed to pick up on their screens was a series of illusory dots that kept the German defenders looking the wrong way.

But the real advance guard of the Allied invasion was already in place. Two days earlier the British had sent out two midget submarines, the X20 and X23, whose task was to mark the points in front of the British beaches where the amphibious tanks were to be lowered into the sea. These tiny craft had

been lying on the sea bottom just off the German-held coast, their crews waiting patiently for the Allied fleet to arrive. When X23 finally surfaced at dawn on D-Day its captain, Lieutenant George Honour, saw the most fantastic sight: the invasion fleet as the Germans were to see it, with ships and landing craft filling the sea to the horizon. It was a sight that Lieutenant Honour would never forget.

CHAPTER ELEVEN

Airborne Attack

ASSAULT FROM THE SKY

While the great phalanx of ships and small craft crept slowly across the Channel, bearing with it the main invasion army, the assault upon Hitler's 'Fortress Europe' had already begun. It came from the sky.

Shortly after midnight on D-Day wave after wave of aircraft and towed gliders set out from England. On board were the elite shock troops of the Allied army of liberation – the three airborne divisions. The airborne assault was an absolutely crucial part of the OVERLORD plan, for it was on the ability of these highly trained men to seize vital bridges and other key objectives inland that the ultimate success of the invasion depended. It was an operation, moreover, fraught with great risks, as the Allied air commanders knew full well. Previous experience of airdrops (the landing of parachute troops and gliders) had shown how difficult it was to drop the troops on target, especially in darkness and in windy conditions. As it turned out, D-Day was to be no exception.

THE AMERICAN AIRDROP

The two American divisions to be dropped in Normandy early on D-Day morning were the 82nd and 101st Airborne. The 82nd, known by its double A badge as the All-American, was commanded by Major General Matthew B. Ridgway. The 101st, whose white eagle badge earned it the nickname the Screaming Eagles, was led by Major General Maxwell Taylor. Both divisions were dropped at 1.30am in the southeast corner of the Cotentin Peninsula, immediately north of the town of Carentan. The 82nd's role was to clear the area west of the Merderet River and seize the village of Ste Mère-Eglise just east of the river and 10 km (6 miles) inshore from UTAH beach. The task of the 101st was to seize and hold the important causeways across the flooded areas behind the beaches so that the seaborne forces, when they arrived, would be able to penetrate inland.

82ND AIRBORNE

Unfortunately, things did not go at all as planned. Many aircraft drifted off course, others lost track of their intended dropping zones, while in many cases the inexperienced pilots of the transport planes took fright at the first signs of German anti-aircraft fire and, diving and weaving through the cloud, spilled out their paratroops indiscriminately. As a result, the American airdrop was little short of chaotic. The troops became scattered over a 48-km (30-mile) area, some finding themselves in areas the Allies did not expect to reach until at least a week later, not having an inkling of where they were or where their commanders were. Some men found themselves quite alone, isolated from their comrades, and wandered around in the darkness.

SETBACKS

Many Americans went through a nightmare ordeal. One group landed smack in the centre of a German command post and were at once captured. Some had their parachutes caught in trees and hung helpless, unable to move. One man nearly suffocated on plunging head first into a haystack. But possibly the worst experience of a paratrooper was that of

Right: Major General Richard Gale, commander of the British 6th Airborne Division, chatting to paratroopers before they emplane on the evening of 5 June 1944 D-Day eve.

a young American, Private John Steele, whose parachute became hooked on the steeple of the church of Ste Mère-Eglise. He hung there terrified while Germans and Americans fired at each other in the darkness of the streets below and occasional streams of machine-gun bullets flashed past his head. Miraculously, Steele survived. He was later cut down by the Germans and taken prisoner.

Of those regiments of the 82nd that were supposed to land west of the Merderet River, only a fraction came down in their allotted area. Three days later the division still had not assembled more than a third of its men. However, one regiment, roughly 1,000-strong, did manage to land fairly accurately in its dropping zone east of the river. Assembling rapidly, a group from this regiment stormed into the streets of Ste Mère-Eglise to the bewilderment of the German defenders. By dawn, after a spirited action, they had captured this important village, blocking the

main highway between Carentan and Cherbourg. Soon the Stars and Stripes was fluttering proudly from the little town hall of Ste Mère-Eglise – the first place of any size to be liberated on D-Day.

General Maxwell Taylor's 101st Division meanwhile had dropped somewhat southeast of the 82nd in wet orchards and hedge-bordered fields, which made assembly difficult since there were no recognizable landmarks. Their only stroke of luck was that they had hit an area where the number of German troops was relatively small. The Americans used a hand-held clicking device as a recognition signal, which doubtless saved many lives. However, before the night was over the Germans had captured some of the clickers and used them to lure the Americans into their field of fire.

Despite the fact that they could muster only a small part of their force, the 101st began to strike determinedly at their given objectives.

STE MERE-EGLISE

101ST AIRBORNE

By dawn the Screaming Eagles had successfully taken the western exits of all the flooded sections behind UTAH beach. Elsewhere small groups of paratroops, operating without command, fought bitter skirmishes with German troops. Others, often assisted by local French Resistance forces, went to work cutting the telephone lines, thereby helping to paralyse the crucial German communications network and creating the maximum confusion among the defenders, who, in most cases, hugely outnumbered the Americans.

A HIGH TOLL

The toll among the Americans that night was heavy. At Ste Mère-Eglise alone more than 150 men were killed and 350 wounded. Many men drowned on parachuting straight into the flooded areas. Losses among the glider-borne troops, who followed the paratroops, were particulary heavy. Some of the Horsa and Hadrian gliders virtually broke up on landing, killing men before they could scramble out of the fuselage.

GERMAN CONFUSION

However, the haphazard nature of the airdrop thoroughly confused the Germans precisely because the landings did not conform to any set pattern. And the aggressiveness and initiative of small groups of paratroopers pinned down the German 91st Division along the Merderet river, preventing it from advancing eastward to the coast. The subsequent landing of the seaborne forces on UTAH beach was thereby assured.

THE BRITISH AIRDROP

6TH AIRBORNE

As the American airborne forces were battling it out in the fields of the Cotentin Peninsula, 80 km (50 miles) to the east the British aerial assault on Normandy was already under way. The British 6th Airborne Division under the command of Major General Richard Gale had been assigned the most vital D-Day mission. The division (whose badge was Pegasus, the winged horse of Greek mythology) had orders to seize and hold the bridges over the River Orne and the Orne Canal between the town of Caen and the sea. In addition they were to knock out the key German coastal battery at Merville, just east of the Orne mouth, to prevent it from firing upon SWORD beach, where the British seaborne troops were due to land. Gale's men were also to try to destroy five bridges across the River Dives, which flows into the sea at Cabourg 10 km (6 miles) east of the Orne. In short, the British division was charged with the responsibility for securing the eastern flank of the Allied bridgehead, where a thrust by the German panzer divisions east of Caen was most likely to come. Failure to hold the line of the Orne would be disastrous, for it would enable the enemy to eliminate the slender bridgehead before the main Allied seaborne divisions could consolidate their foothold. This threat from the German armour was what Eisenhower and Montgomery feared most of all.

To carry out his formidable task Gale devised a daring plan. Knowing that the bridges across the Orne had demolition charges placed in them by the Germans, he decided that they could be captured intact only by a swift surprise attack. His plan was to crash-land 200 infantry troops and engineers onto the defences of the two main bridges and seize them before the Germans knew what was happening. At the same time Gale aimed to land 60 men of the 22nd Independent Parachute Company to act as pathfinders, setting up lights and beacons to mark the correct dropping zones for the main follow-up parachute brigades.

THE ORNE BRIDGES

The success of this bold operation depended on speed of action and split-second timing. The first part of it, the seizure of the canal and Orne bridges, was carried out in brilliant style. Six gliders, carrying five platoons of the Oxford and Buckinghamshire Light Infantry and 30 men of the 249th Field Company, Royal Engineers, hurtled down

Left: The airborne assault. American gliders crash land in the fields of the Cotentin peninsula, west of UTAH beach. Other gliders are circling in the air before swooping down to land. One glider (middle left) can be seen with its fuselage fully broken in half.

We formed into a very tight formation. Through broken clouds and a bright moon we headed for the coast. Over the Channel you could see hundreds of boats starting towards the Continent. I had the feeling we were part of a big chunk of history. Looking out of the window in every direction were planes. About 1am, June 6, one of the guys yelled 'There she is boys.' We all knew what it was – the coast of France. At 9 minutes to drop zone, flak and machine gun tracers could be seen to the right and left. It looked just like the Fourth of July. About that moment a plane on our right blew up, hit the ground in a large ball of fire, 18 to 20 men wiped out. This was no Fourth of July celebration. Welcome to the real war.

The red light in the door came on. We stood up and hooked up. Then the green light, and we were out of the door. Quite a struggle because of all our equipment. Someone fell down and had to be helped up and out the door. When I jumped it looked like every tracer in the sky was zeroing in on me. I'm sure the rest of the guys felt the same way. I don't know how high our plane was, but I'm sure it was very low because I remember swinging about twice and then hitting in the middle of a road. I could see a man and a woman standing in the front yard of a house just beneath me. I hit the road, took about two steps, and went head first through a wicket fence, knocking out two teeth and cutting my lip. I rolled over, tried to get my carbine out, couldn't, sat up, and the man and woman were gone. I finally got out of my harness, pulled my folding stock carbine out and could hear some soldiers coming down the road. I started up a hedgerow but it felt like someone was holding me by the belt. I stopped, tried to move again, same thing. I slowly turned around and found the shroud lines from my parachute were tangled up in the fence. I could hear the boots getting closer and closer. I finally got the shroud lines unhooked, climbed to the top of the hedgerow, fell over on the other side, and in about a minute 35 or 40 Germans came marching past where I had just been. I could have reached out and touched them. After they passed by I moved in the direction I thought our plane had come in. Being alone behind enemy lines is a unique, indescribable feeling. You just feel so helpless, so alone.

George M. Rosie, 101st Airborne Division

right on schedule half an hour after midnight. One glider went astray, but the remaining five were on target. They skated into land at more than 160 kmph (100 mph) smashing through the barbed-wire defences. They broke up on landing and the troops poured out of the wrecked fuselages and rushed the bridges. The startled Germans barely had time to train a machine gun on the attackers before it was all over. The bridge over the canal at Bénouville (now known as Pegasus Bridge) and the river bridge at Ranville were in British hands within fifteen minutes.

The pathfinders, meanwhile, had been blown east of the intended dropping zone by the high winds. As a result the paratroops who were to reinforce the tiny group holding the Orne bridges came down some distance away. In spite of the scattered nature of the drop, the 5th Parachute Brigade succeeded in driving the Germans out of the village of Ranville, just east of the river, before 4.30am. General Gale had the satisfaction of setting up his headquarters there while antitank guns from the newly landed glider force were rushed forward to protect the village from the expected armoured counterattack.

RANVILLE

The most difficult task for the British airborne troops was the capture of the Merville battery. It was entrusted to one battalion of the 3rd Parachute Brigade led by Lieutenant Colonel Terence Otway. Otway, a Sandhurst-trained professional soldier, found to his horror that everything was going wrong. First, he landed badly in a farmyard after German troops had riddled his parachute with gunfire and he barely had time to struggle out of his harness and run before enemy troops rushed out of the farmhouse. Otway then discovered that only 150 of his 800 men had mustered. The rest, as was happening with the Americans, had been scattered far and wide in the gusting winds. Worse still, the battalion had lost nearly all its mine detectors, mortars and antitank guns.

MERVILLE

Undaunted, a reconnaissance party cut the outer wire defences of the German battery and crawled through the inner minefield in the dark. Having lost their marker tapes, they marked the safe trail by using their feet only. Otway's men then launched a desperate assault on the German position. Braving heavy machine-gun fire, they rushed forward from trench to trench and, after a savage hand-to-hand struggle, forced open the German artillery casemates and destroyed the guns. By 4.45am this fragment of a battalion had captured the Merville battery and Otway duly sent the news to England by carrier pigeon. Nearly half of his intrepid little force was killed or wounded in the action.

The rest of the 3rd Brigade suffered much the same fate as the paratroops of the American 82nd. They were strung out over the land lying between the valleys of the Orne and the Dives, much of which had been deliberately flooded. Hundreds dropped in the flooded waters of the Dives or among the trees of the Bois de Bavent 10 km (6 miles) northeast of Caen. Many drowned, some were taken prisoner, others disappeared, never to be found. Amazingly, those who did land safely succeeded in blowing up all five of the bridges over the Dives. The most important was the bridge at Troarn 11 km (7 miles) east of Caen on the Route Nationale 175, a bridge across which enemy armoured reinforcements from the east would have to come. In a daring expedition Major Rosveare, accompanied by seven sappers, commandeered a Royal Army Medical Corps jeep and drove like a madman down the road into Troarn, shot at all the time by astonished Germans. Rosveare and his men set the charge and blew up the bridge under the noses of the enemy and returned safely to the British-held sector. The rest of the 6th Airborne meanwhile cleared both banks of the River Orne and held the river line until they were relieved later on D-Day morning by a British commando brigade landing from the sea.

TROARN BRIDGE

Left: General Eisenhower bidding good luck to paratroopers of the US 101st Airborne Division on the eve of the invasion. The men already have their faces blackened in readiness for the night drop.

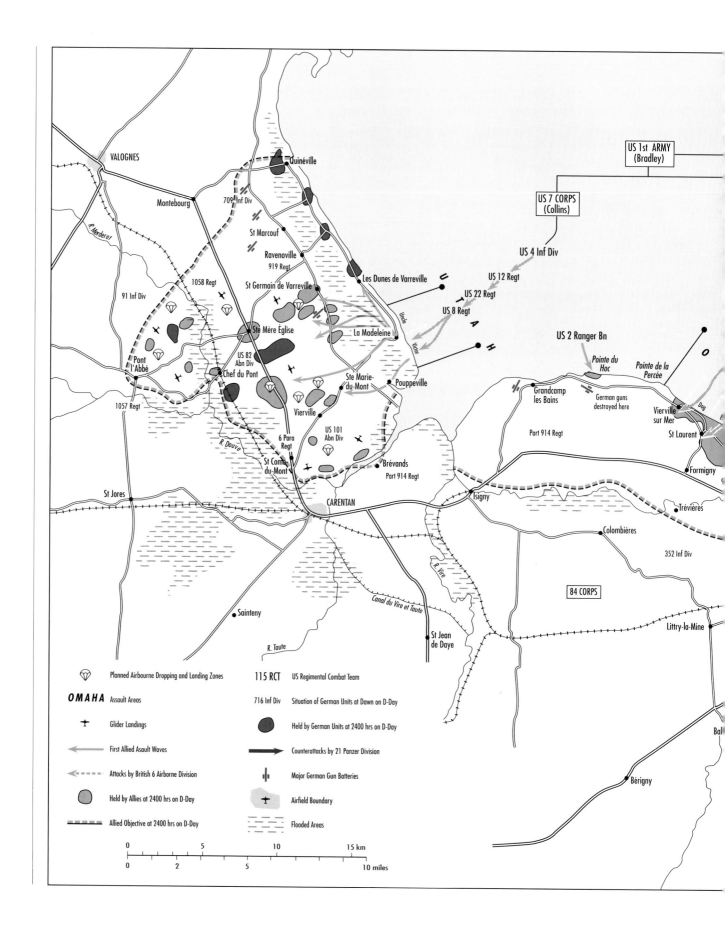

US 1st ARMY
(Bradley)

US 7 CORPS
(Collins)

US 4 Inf Div

US 12 Regt

US 22 Regt

US 8 Regt

US 2 Ranger Bn

VALOGNES

Quinéville

Montebourg

709 Inf Div

St Marcouf

Ravenoville

919 Regt

Les Dunes de Varreville

St Germain de Varreville

1058 Regt

91 Inf Div

Ste Mère Église

U T A H

La Madeleine

Pointe du Hoc

Pointe de la Percée

US 82
Abn Div

Pont
l'Abbé

Chef du Pont

Ste Marie-
du-Mont

Pouppeville

Grandcamp
les Bains

German guns
destroyed here

Vierville
sur Mer

St Laurent

Uncle

Victor

1057 Regt

Vierville

US 101
Abn Div

Part 914 Regt

Formigny

6 Para
Regt

St Come-
du-Mont

Brévands

Part 914 Regt

St Jores

CARENTAN

Isigny

Trévières

R. Merderet

R. Douve

Colombières

352 Inf Div

Sainteny

R. Vire

84 CORPS

Littry-la-Mine

St Jean
de Daye

Canal du Vire et Taute

R. Taute

Bérigny

Bal

Dog

O

Symbol	Description
Planned Airbourne Dropping and Landing Zones	
OMAHA	Assault Areas
+	Glider Landings
→	First Allied Asault Waves
← - - -	Attacks by British 6 Airborne Division
●	Held by Allies at 2400 hrs on D-Day
▬ ▬ ▬	Allied Objective at 2400 hrs on D-Day

Symbol	Description
115 RCT	US Regimental Combat Team
716 Inf Div	Situation of German Units at Dawn on D-Day
●	Held by German Units at 2400 hrs on D-Day
➤	Counterattacks by 21 Panzer Division
⊣⊢	Major German Gun Batteries
✈	Airfield Boundary
≈≈≈	Flooded Areas

0   5   10   15 km

0   2   5   10 miles

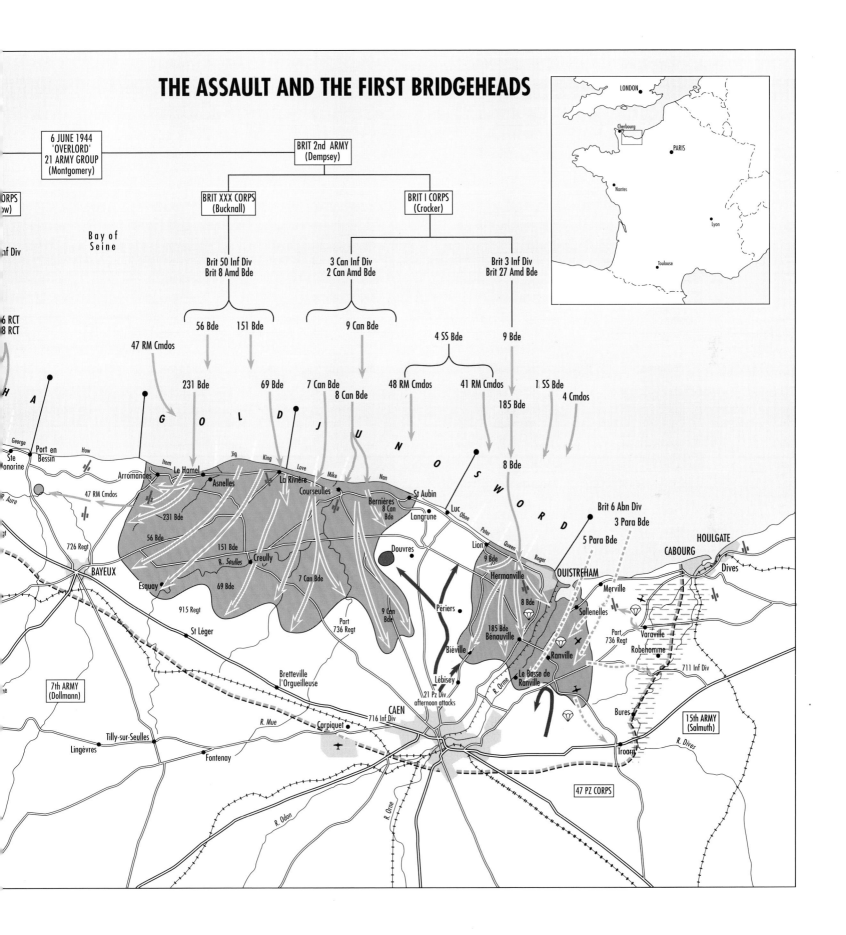

THE ASSAULT AND THE FIRST BRIDGEHEADS

CHAPTER TWELVE

The American Landings: UTAH

Right: American troops wade ashore from landing craft off UTAH beach.

Dawn on D-Day morning. Grey clouds and a choppy sea. Along the French coast from the Cotentin Peninsula to the mouth of the Orne at Ouistreham the vast invasion fleet was by now in position. Far out at sea flashes of gunfire came as the Allied warships opened up in a massive bombardment of the coastal defences. At the same time hundreds of Allied aircraft swept in low across the coast to pound the German strongpoints. Along UTAH beach on the southeast corner of the Cotentin, where the first landings were to be made, the American battleship *Nevada* and the cruisers *Quincy* and *Tuscaloosa* poured their shells onto the German batteries ranged along the distant shoreline. They were joined by the British cruisers HMS *Black Prince*, HMS *Hawkins*, HMS *Enterprise* and a dozen destroyers. Soon the German guns from St Vaast-la-Hougue to Vierville opened up in reply.

Against the background of this ear-splitting bombardment the first assault craft, carrying two battalions of the US 4th Infantry Division, headed in towards the shore. These men were the spearhead of the Allied seaborne force. They formed the assault wave of the US 7th Corps commanded by Lieutenant

General J. Lawton Collins – a popular commander known to the GIs as Lightning Joe. In the murky grey light, the landing craft began to disgorge their troops precisely on time, which at UTAH was 6.30am. The troops waded some 90m (300ft) to the beach. With them came 28 of the amphibious DD tanks, which began firing to cover the men as soon as they jumped out of the landing craft. Four more DD tanks were unfortunately lost offshore when the LCT carrying them struck a mine. The appearance of the tanks undoubtedly had a shattering effect upon the German defenders, who were astonished to see armoured vehicles emerging from the sea.

6.30AM

As the American infantry moved inshore across the sand dunes to breach the defences of the sea wall, Army engineers rapidly set to work to clear the beach obstacles. By sheer good luck a navigational error had brought the troops onto a beach approximately 1.5 km (1 mile) south of where they were supposed to land. Only one enemy battalion of low grade troops was stationed in this sector because the Germans believed that the heavily flooded area behind the beach would deter any attempt at landing there. As a result the American assault troops encountered

Left: H-Hour at UTAH. Assault spearheads of the US 4th Infantry Division jump from their landing craft into the sea. The UTAH landing went ahead with surprising ease against only light initial opposition.

A memorial poem dedicated to the men of the 82nd Airborne Division who gave their lives at Ste Mère-Eglise

IN MEMORY

We leave them here at Mère-Eglise
Among the Norman flowers,
We wish they could go back with us
To those British friends of ours.

But all who face the enemy
Cannot return back home,
Some had to pay the price supreme
Across the channel foam.

They may have died in drop from plane
Upon the Norman Green,
Or died because a glider crashed
At H plus seventeen,

They may have fought for 131
Or on 95 have died,
No matter where they gave their lives
They rest here side by side.

We only hope that folks back home,
Where peace and quiet reign,
Appreciate the life they gave
Upon the Norman plain.

We trust their souls have gone above
Where all is rest and peace,
And bodies will turn back to dust
Here at Ste Mère-Eglise.

                              Milton Chadwick

This was written near La Haye-de-Puits during a short break in the bloodiest battle the author was in. He and his surviving comrades of the 82nd Airborne Division had just received notice that at some later date they would be pulled from battle and return to England. At this same time near Ste Mère-Eglise, they were burying some of the friends he had known and lived with for 2 years.

only slight opposition, and they duly turned north along the beach to attack the much more strongly held German fortifications between La Madeleine and Les Dunes de Varreville. There the German opposition became much tougher.

The first person to size up accurately the situation developing on UTAH was the deputy commander of the 4th Division, Brigadier General Theodore Roosevelt Jr, the son of former US President 'Teddy' Roosevelt. At 57 the General, an astute and experienced soldier, was considered too old for front-line action, but had persuaded his superiors to let

Right: Men of the US 8th Infantry Regiment crossing the sea wall behind UTAH beach and climbing the dunes to penetrate inland.

We fly down the sandy coastline, just over the water's edge. The flak is coming thick now, for we are approaching the target. The big red blobs split between us and the wing man, and that, my good friends, is too close. I suddenly seize an extra helmet and sit upon it. I wish to God those bombs were gone.

Somehow I try to pull my head down into the flak suit, knowing full well that it's not much protection, that a fragment of shell goes through as if it were paper. I stare down first right and then left, and just then two boats go up in explosions. Apparently they must have hit mines, but they're well beyond our approaching armada.

German E-boats are firing at us now near shore. Puffs of black shell smoke hang farther back. I do not see it, but one puts an incendiary into a bomber, sets it on fire. Three of the boys bail out into the water.

The pilot tries to get his bombs to the target. He struggles with the crippled aeroplane, then in a flash it blows to pieces. The fire had ignited the bomb-load. That is the only loss our group has. Now inland about half a mile there is a terrible commotion. A patch of hellish smoke and fire bubbles skywards.

Flak bursts all around, but I pay no attention. Over the phone comes the call: 'Bombs away!' We are approaching that battery of Nazi guns. They look like a series of golf bunkers, neatly ranged like some sandy folly on the beach. I see the racks suddenly empty, the bombs fall down.

Our wave was over the beaches in about 20 minutes, during which time we bombed every gun installation assigned to us. We flew up the peninsula and circled the island of Guernsey, where we watched destroyers working over the island. They were doing a beautiful job of it.

Extract from the diary of Lieutenant Colonel James Norgaard of the 344th Bomb Group, USAAF. The 344th led the 600 planes of the 9th Air Force to bomb behind UTAH beach.

Left: American troops in dug out positions in the sands of UTAH beach, ready to protect the follow-up forces coming ashore. Jeeps and tanks are dotted along the shoreline.

A CHANGE OF PLAN

Right: A German defender lies dead outside his pill box on UTAH beach.

him go ashore with the first wave. He quickly realized that attempts to push northwards up the beach in the face of heavy German fire were useless and that the best course would be for the division to abandon its planned objectives and instead exploit the lucky chance that had brought it onto the wrong beach. That meant that the men should strike directly inland across the weakly defended causeways, so opening the way for the follow-up troops and armour, which could land on a beach that was now relatively safe. General Roosevelt thereupon reorganized his troops, who soon began to infiltrate west-wards towards Audouville-la-Hubert, on the far side of the flooded sector. At the same time

Left: The Far Shore at last! American infantry spilling down the ramps of their assault craft get their first close up view of the enemy coast.

another battalion turned south, heading for the coastal hamlet of Pouppeville, which was shortly to come under attack by a small party of troops of the 101st Airborne. General Roosevelt's prompt action played a signal part in ensuring the success of the UTAH landing, and was to earn him the United States Medal of Honor.

By mid-morning units of the 4th Division made contact with airborne troops near Pouppeville and the hamlet was soon in American hands. Others were pushing inland to relieve the hard-pressed men of the 82nd Airborne Division, who were holding out against a strong German counterattack at Ste Mère-Eglise. On UTAH beach itself the follow-up forces were pouring ashore. The Western Task Force, positioned well offshore, was

moving wave after wave of landing craft onto the cleared beaches. By afternoon some 21,000 troops and 2,000 vehicles had been landed together with a massive amount of supplies and ammunition. The American lodgement on the Cotentin Peninsula was getting stronger by the minute.

By nightfall on D-Day the American 7th Corps was in control of the territory between the coast and the Merderet River to a depth of about 8 km (5 miles). The Americans had not taken all their objectives and were meeting stiff resistance on the northern edge of their narrow front, but they had prised open this key section of Hitler's Atlantic Wall with the loss of no more than 200 lives. In the light of this outcome, UTAH had to be counted a major Allied triumph.

OUTCOME

CHAPTER THIRTEEN

The American Landings: OMAHA

Right: OMAHA – the near disaster. Robert Capa's classic photograph of an American soldier edging grimly ashore under fire in the shallows off OMAHA beach. Steel crisscross 'hedgehog' obstacles project from the sea-covered sands behind. Hundreds died in the water as the Germans unleashed a merciless hail of fire.

SEA SICKNESS

While the UTAH landing was going ahead surprisingly smoothly, 20 km (13 miles) to the east on OMAHA beach the Americans were running into serious trouble. Almost everything about this second American landing went badly wrong. First, the assault battalions were loaded into their landing craft from the transport ships about 19 km (12 miles) out from the coast. In the rough and choppy conditions prevailing, this decision was undoubtedly a serious blunder. Most of the men soon became seasick. By the end of the long run-in many were too weak and

wretched to be able to stand up, let alone fight. The turbulent sea swamped several craft almost as soon as they touched the water. Worse still, the amphibious DD tanks, which were launched as much as 6 km (4 miles) from the beach, encountered conditions they were never designed to cope with. Clumsy vehicles at best, they could only function properly in calm shallow water. As a result a number sank like stones, drowning their crews; others foundered on the long approach run. Of the 30 DD tanks launched in the first wave only two reached the shore.

The biggest mistake, however, was the

DD TANKS LOST

overall assault plan. The landing was to be carried out by troops of the United States 5th Corps, commanded by Major General Leonard Gerow. The Corps comprised the 1st and 29th Infantry Divisions, of which the 1st, commanded by Major General C.R. Huebner, was to make the initial assault. Huebner had been ordered to carry out what amounted to a direct frontal attack on a beach that was particularly heavily fortified. OMAHA was a concave-shaped beach, roughly 6 km (4 miles) long, with steep cliffs at each end. The land between was gently sloping, intersected by several little valleys which provided the only way off the sandy beach. The Germans had their main strongpoints with artillery, mortars and machine guns on the cliffs. Along the beach itself were a succession of minefields and the exit valleys were heavily mined and booby-trapped. The Americans had assumed that the beach was manned by just one regiment of the 716th Division, a medium-grade German division which guarded the central part of the Normandy coast. In fact a second division of battle-hardened troops, the 352nd, was also close at hand. The Americans therefore had little idea of how strongly defended the OMAHA sector really was. Neither did they realize how formidable the gun emplacements were. Some German gun casemates were 6m (20ft) thick, concrete redoubts reinforced with steel and with magazines and living quarters deep underground. The American commanders believed that by landing their strongest forces right in front of these strongpoints they would be able to take them by storm. But the plan led to near disaster.

The first assault craft moved in on the western end of OMAHA beach at 6.30am. This stretch of beach had been given the code name Dog Green. Although the German defences had been heavily bombed and shelled beforehand, the bombardment had had little effect. The German gunners, unscathed inside their

Right: General Omar Bradley watches anxiously aboard Admiral Kirk's flagship, the cruiser USS *Augusta*, as the assult on OMAHA gets under way. For more than six hours the situation on OMAHA remained touch and go and the landing was nearly called off.

6.30AM: DOG GREEN

pillboxes and concrete bastions, were waiting and ready. The moment that the leading company of Americans from the 116th Infantry Regiment hit the beach and leaped from their landing craft they were met by a vicious hail of mortar and machine-gun fire. Men simply crumpled and fell.

From then on it was a struggle for survival. The troops, unable to move, crawled to find shelter in the shallows behind steel obstacles. Some Americans who were unhurt tried desperately to drag wounded comrades from the water to save them from drowning. By the time the next flotilla of landing craft came in half an hour later, the remnants of the first assault companies were still pinned down on the water's edge.

The carnage on Dog Green was repeated with varying degrees of severity right along OMAHA beach from Vierville-sur-Mer in the west to Colleville in the east. On the beach named Easy Red, which was subjected to murderous fire from the German batteries, the American troops were so demoralized that they could only huddle helplessly under the cover of the sea wall, where many had already died. An American Colonel is recorded as having stood up and, looking down on them disgustedly, declared: 'There's only two kinds of men who are going to stay on this beach – the dead and those who are about to die. Now let's get the hell out of here.' The troops plucked up courage and obeyed. Another who played a legendary role in rallying the men was Brigadier General Norman Cota of the 29th Division (the Blue and Gray). Displaying complete contempt for the enemy fire, Cota strode undaunted up and down the shoreline urging the men to get off the beach and up the bluffs.

Many landing craft came in well to the east of their intended beach and this caused great confusion. Several were hit on the run-in, one sinking less than 1 km ($\frac{1}{2}$ mile) from the shore. The men on board, leaping into the sea, were pulled under by their heavy combat gear and drowned. All momentum was lost because of the intensity and accuracy of the enemy fire. On shore men picked their way slowly off the beaches and moved cautiously in single file up the narrow exit paths, terrified lest they set foot on a mine. Wounded men lay where they fell and their comrades stepped over them as to move off the track meant certain death. In one company 47 men died while groping their way along a mine-infested path towards Colleville. Meanwhile the beaches were becoming congested as more men and

EASY RED

COTA

CONGESTION ON BEACH

Right: American infantry come ashore at OMAHA after the initial assault. A line of troops advances up a mine-cleared track inshore. Amphibious DUKW trucks and half tracks towing antitank guns hug the shoreline.

Left: The chaos and confusion along this beach as US troops, some of them wounded, struggle ashore. The German gun emplacements ran along the cliffs behind the beach. Wrecked vehicles litter this shoreline.

vehicles arrived. Urgently needed tanks and heavy guns could not be landed because there was simply not enough room. The engineers, who suffered particularly heavy casualties, were still struggling to clear paths through the beach minefields so that the men huddled between the shingle and the water's edge could penetrate inland.

For six hours the situation on OMAHA remained critical. All along the shoreline was a confused jumble of wreckage: smashed landing craft, burning tanks and dead bodies. Offshore, aboard his command cruiser USS *Augusta*, General Bradley watched in anguish as the battle raged. He waited, taut with apprehension, while the reports from his shore commanders came through. At one point the situation was so grave that he was on the point of signalling Montgomery to request that the assault be halted and the follow-up regiments transferred to the British beaches further east. But finally, early that

afternoon, Bradley received his first reassuring message: 'Troops formerly pinned down on Easy Red, Easy Green and Fox Red advancing up the heights beyond the beaches.'

What saved the OMAHA landing from being a total disaster was unquestionably the immense courage and initiative shown by individual groups of American infantrymen. Amid the inferno of exploding shells and machine gun fire small parties of men worked their way gradually inshore and round the back of the German gun emplacements. Often leaderless and without radio communication, they fought what amounted to a savage guerrilla-type action. At the western end of the beach troops of the 29th Division succeeded in taking the village of Vierville. To the east, units of the 1st Division had reached the outskirts of Colleville, 1.5 km (1 mile) inland, although the Germans fought fiercely to hold the village and were not dislodged until the following day. In the

BRADLEY'S ANGUISH

COURAGE AND INITIATIVE

VIERVILLE

Right: A makeshift casualty station under the cliffs near Colleville on D-Day. Wounded men of the 16th Infantry Regiment receive medical attention.

OMAHA

It was 7.30am when we neared the marker for our entrance. At this time we got hit and quite a few men were burnt. We got hit again by 88-mm shells. By this time the Engineers came on deck to disembark but we were nowhere near the beach. We all crawled to the back of the craft and men were already jumping overboard. The water was cold and the second thing I realized was that my equipment was too heavy. I took off my pack and medical pouches and struggled to get off my gas mask. I came across Captain Albert and Smitty. All this time 88's were aiming at us in the water and there was machine gun fire from the hill off the beach. Men who couldn't swim or were afraid of the water managed to hold onto obstacles which were mined. Some went off either by pressure of the man or from machine gun fire, I don't know which.

The water was rough and only with the help of the waves could we get near the shore. It was still over our heads when I felt a hard blow and heard a loud noise. Captain Albert just disappeared. I didn't notice Smitty until after I got up for I'd been knocked out and didn't know if I was hit or not. Smitty was holding my hand, asking me to take him in, and then I noticed that he was hit for he had shrapnel wounds all over his face. Every time the waves went out I saw blood coming up the water from Smitty's lower body. He started to cry that he didn't want to drown. I cannot express my feelings but I'm sure I cried too, for here was my first taste of war. Smitty said: 'Take me in, Sol. I'm losing a lot of blood'. Honest, I must have swallowed a quart of his blood. His voice got weaker all the time. Finally I touched bottom and we walked very slowly. Smitty was getting weaker and I had to half carry him. The stones went up the beach for about 10 feet and there was a wooden structure on the side of a little incline. That's where all the men were. As we got out of the water my feet wouldn't hold me. The further I got on the beach, the heavier Smitty was getting. He passed out and finally a Ranger Lieutenant ran down, exposing himself to fire, and helped me drag him up to the stones. I started shivering and nothing could stop me. I sat up and Smitty's head was in my lap when he died.

Sergeant Sol Evnetzky, 147th Combat Engineer Battalion

central part of OMAHA, on beaches Easy Red and Easy Green, two battalions rushed the beach defences under covering fire from Allied destroyers that steamed in close to the beach. One by one the German strongpoints were knocked out or captured. But the heavy German shelling of the beach continued right through until the evening. By nightfall, however, the German shoreline defences began slowly to crumble and the fire from the gun emplacements slackened. Ammunition was beginning to run low. US artillery was being landed to support the forward infantry and almost the whole of Gerow's 5th Corps was now ashore and working at full speed to widen the cleared gaps in the minefields.

At the end of D-Day the Americans on OMAHA controlled a beachhead approximately 10 km (6 miles) long and a mere 3 km (2 miles) deep at its furthest point. It was, at best, a shaky foothold and was to remain for several days the most vulnerable sector of the

NIGHTFALL

A SHAKY FOOTHOLD

Allied invasion front. A determined German counterattack would very likely have swept the US Corps back into the sea. Fortunately, no such attack came. So confident had the Germans been that the American landing was being repelled that they had switched their reserves from the OMAHA sector to reinforce their troops in the British sector.

HEAVY LOSSES

The OMAHA assault on D-Day itself cost the Americans roughly 3,000 dead and wounded. In addition 50 tanks and the same number of landing craft were destroyed together with 10 larger vessels.

General Bradley later paid tribute to the men of the 1st US Infantry Division, who had spearheaded the OMAHA landing. Veterans of the Sicily landings a year earlier, they were known from their divisional number emblem as the Big Red One. 'Had a less experienced division stumbled into this crack resistance', Bradley wrote, 'it might easily have been thrown back into the Channel.'

THE BIG RED ONE

POINTE DU HOC – THE MYSTERY OF THE GUNS

In addition to UTAH and OMAHA there was a third American landing on D-Day morning, and it turned out to be one of the epic actions of that historic day.

Some 8 km (5 miles) west of OMAHA the Germans were believed to have installed a powerful coastal battery on top of a rocky promontory called the Pointe Du Hoc. The

Right: A wounded GI is treated by a medical officer after the landing.

battery, as the Allied commanders realized, would be able to fire upon both UTAH and OMAHA beaches and it was considered vital that it be put out of action without delay. This incredibly dangerous task was assigned to a small crack force of US Rangers (the American equivalent of British commandos) under the command of Lieutenant Colonel James E. Rudder. The Rangers, 225 men in all, were expected to climb an almost sheer cliff about 30m (100ft) high, overcome the German defenders and destroy the guns. After a preliminary bombardment by the US battleship *Texas* and escorted by two destroyers – the USS *Satterlee* and HMS *Talybont* – the Rangers landed on the narrow

beach at the foot of the cliff and prepared to scale the heights under fire. Using grappling hooks and rope ladders, they swarmed up the cliff face while the Germans hurled down grenades and fired at them with machine guns. Some Americans fell to their deaths when the Germans cut the ropes. But the Rangers kept on coming, and after a frenzied effort they managed to reach the summit in numbers and stormed the German position, which was one of the strongest emplacements along the Atlantic Wall. When they got there the heroic band of Americans found that the concrete casemates were wrecked and that the guns they had come to destroy were not there. It was a bitter disappointment. Their

RUDDER

Left: The Stars and Stripes displayed proudly on the Pointe du Hoc after its capture by troops of the 2nd Ranger Battalion. German prisoners are led out of the ruined emplacements. The Rangers' assault on this heavily defended position was one of the most outstanding Allied actions of the D-Day invasion.

Left: Beached landing craft and debris strewn along the water's edge following the landings. Larger transport and supply ships can be seen waiting offshore.

The Pointe du Hoc – how the German guns were found and destroyed

I took my platoon sergeant, Jack Kuhn, with me to go and scout around to see what lay further inland and we stumbled on the gun emplacement where the coastal guns had been moved to their alternative position. And there they were – the five of them – sitting in a little valley all in position and not a shell crater near them. The ammunition depot was nearby. We looked over the top of the hedgerow and saw that they were unattended. It was 8.30 am. Their troops were about 100 yards away, being talked to by their officers. So my friend just stayed there on top of the hedgerow with a sub-machine-gun to cover me while I went in and destroyed the guns. I laid thermite grenades in their traversing and elevation mechanisms and in their breech blocks. And practically noiselessly I pulled the pin and this melted their gears into molten metal and I then destroyed their sights. They were just melted metal when I got through with them, totally inoperable. Kuhn and I withdrew as fast as we could back to our platoon road block a few hundred yards away. Although the Germans started to move towards the guns, I don't think they saw us.

Leonard G. Lomell, First Sergeant, later Lieutenant,
D Company, 2nd Ranger Battalion US Army

brave assault, it seemed, had been in vain.

However, half an hour later, two Rangers scouting inland spotted what they rightly took to be the missing battery – five 155 mm guns – repositioned in a little valley with their crews nearby. The guns were apparently targeted towards UTAH beach to the west. One soldier kept watch while the other, First Sergeant Leonard Lomell, crept into the valley unobserved and destroyed the guns single-handed. The Rangers, who suffered heavy casualties, had achieved their objective after all; and Lomell, who sustained a bullet wound in the side earlier during the landing, was later awarded the American Distinguished Service Cross for his action. Why the Germans had failed to site the guns in their prepared position on the cliff top is a D-Day mystery that has never been satisfactorily explained.

Colonel Rudder's little force held their position despite German counterattacks for two days until they were relieved by units of the 5th Ranger Battalion and the 116th Infantry Regiment who reached them from OMAHA. Of the original 225 men, only 90 remained alive.

LOMELL

CHAPTER FOURTEEN

The British Beaches

General Sir Miles Dempsey's British 2nd Army was to make its assault one hour after the American landings, the later time being due to the difference in the tides. It was to be a concerted attack by three divisions, two British, one Canadian. They would be supported by commando units, which had been assigned special tasks.

GOLD

The most westerly of the British beaches, GOLD, extended for some 5 km (3 miles), lying roughly between the coastal villages of Le Hamel and La Rivière. The central beach,

JUNO

JUNO, was of similar length and ran between La Rivière and the hamlet of Luc-sur-Mer. SWORD, the easternmost beach, comprised a shorter stretch of coast between Lion-sur-Mer and the small township of Ouistreham, on the mouth of the Orne. Whereas the beaches allocated to the Americans were rather barren and in peacetime only sparsely populated, the British, by contrast, were to go ashore on what before the war had been a popular French holiday area. La Rivière, Courseulles, Bernières, St Aubin and Lion-sur-Mer were all tiny seaside resorts, as was Riva Bella, adjoining Ouistreham, which had

SWORD

Right: Men of the 48th Royal Marine Commandos coming ashore from landing craft at St Aubin-sur-Mer on Nan sector of JUNO beach. The commandos formed the eastern flank of the Canadian bridgehead.

its own casino. Beach homes, holiday villas and hotels, many of them converted into machine-gun nests and strongpoints, were thickly dotted along the shoreline. Although the British beaches were somewhat easier to attack than OMAHA because of their flatter terrain, they were heavily defended and the Germans were strongly entrenched inland, especially between SWORD beach and Caen.

EASTERN TASK FORCE

Shortly before sunrise on D-Day the Eastern Task Force of Rear Admiral Vian took up its assault stations along the British side of the Bay of the Seine and the guns of the Royal Navy began a massive bombardment of the shore defences. The cruisers *Ajax*, *Argonaut*, *Emerald*, *Orion*, *Belfast* and *Diadem* poured a torrent of shells onto the German batteries behind GOLD and JUNO beaches, while further east the cruisers *Danae*, *Frobisher*, *Arethusa* and the Polish cruiser *Dragon* pounded batteries around the mouth of the Orne. They were joined by the big battleships *Ramillies*

and *Warspite*, whose 15-in guns engaged the German heavy batteries between the Orne and Le Havre at the mouth of the Seine.

To prevent the heavy guns at Le Havre from firing on the assembled fleet the Allies laid down a thick smoke screen. However, before the naval bombardment opened, three German torpedo boats on routine patrol passed through the smoke screen and discovered the Allied armada filling the sea around them. The astonished German patrol commander, Heinrich Hoffmann, at once ordered his boats to attack. They raced in, fired off a flurry of torpedoes and sped back to port to give the alarm. All the torpedoes missed except one, which struck the Norwegian destroyer *Svenner*. Hit amidships, the *Svenner* broke in two and sank immediately, with the loss of 34 lives. This was the only attempt the German navy made to oppose the Allied assault and the *Svenner* was the only Allied ship to be sunk through direct enemy action

Above: High tide at JUNO. Canadian troops equipped with bicycles swarm ashore at Bernières after the initial assault spearheads have cleared the beaches.

SVENNER

Right: British troops of the 1st Battalion, South Lancashire Regiment landing under fire on Queen White sector of SWORD beach near Ouistreham. Wounded men are being helped ashore by comrades. Tanks of the 13th/18th Hussars are seen in the background. SWORD beach remained dangerously exposed to German artillery fire throughout D-Day and for several days afterwards.

OMAHA

When I came to the surface all I could see was just a blur in front of me and I could see guys trying to swim that way. So I went that way too. The next thing I knew I was touching bottom, standing maybe armpit deep in water and the little waves were shoving me back as I walked in. Then I saw what chaos was going on up on the beach and I could hear mortar rounds, possibly artillery shells, hitting up there. I could also hear rifle and machine gun fire. They had some big steel cross things sticking up out of the water and I remember going under one of them and trying to stay behind that steel. There were so many guys around there that I felt kind of guilty trying to stay behind something. So I thought. Well, I could see the beach and a number of fellows lying on the beach and about 35 yards across the beach there were cliffs. And I knew that if I could get under that cliff, at least I'd be safe from small arms fire coming down and possibly from mortar fire. So I finally inched my way up out of the water and all of a sudden I realized how cold I was. Anyway, I jumped up and started running. As I ran along the beach I picked up a rifle. There was a guy lying on the beach with two bandoliers of ammunition in his hand and I took them.

... As we were sitting there, either too scared to get up or not wanting to, a lieutenant colonel came down the beach and nonchalantly walked in and said, 'Who's the noncommissioned officer around here?' I didn't say a word. I didn't see any other noncommissioned officers making any move to get up. And this fellow in my gun crew – if I ever wanted to strangle anyone, it was him – said, 'Here's my sergeant'. This lieutenant colonel turned to me and said, 'Are you a noncommissioned officer?' And I said, 'Yes, I'm a sergeant in the artillery – a chief of section'. The lieutenant colonel said, 'Well, you start gathering these men up, since you are the only sergeant here'. Then he pointed to a place down the beach and added, 'Go down there and see the Lieutenant'. I replied, 'But I'm not an infantryman, I'm an artilleryman'. And he said, 'I don't care what you are. Have you ever had any infantry training?' I said, 'Well, no, but I was in the cavalry once'. And he said, 'That's good enough. You're in the infantry now'.

Jerry W. Eades, 62nd Armored Field Artillery, US Army

on D-Day itself. One American destroyer, the USS *Corry*, sank off UTAH after hitting a mine.

The British transport ships came in much closer than the American transports, anchoring only 13 km (8 miles) offshore, as Admiral Sir Bertram Ramsay had recommended. And this was an undoubted advantage. But for the British and Canadian assault troops, who

CORRY

scrambled down the nets into the pitching landing craft, the run-in through the choppy sea and the deafening shellfire would be almost as unpleasant as for the Americans. With ships' tannoys blaring out popular songs and accompanied by shouts of 'Good luck', 'Remember Dunkirk' and 'Remember Dieppe', the first boats got away and headed

for the distant Normandy shore, half obscured by the dust and smoke of explosions. Huddled together, chilled by the icy spray, the troops cracked jokes to keep up their spirits. Some sang; others remained grimly silent. Each man had his own thoughts and fears about what lay ahead. Suddenly, as the landing craft neared the shore, the naval bombardment lifted. For the troops this was the moment of truth, the moment they had trained for and waited for so expectantly. This was H-Hour. Timed to the exact second, the British assault went in.

H-HOUR

GOLD

The attack on GOLD beach was spearheaded by the 50th (Northumbrian) Division which formed part of Lieutenant General G.C. Bucknall's British XXX Corps. In spite of its name the division comprised regiments drawn from many other parts of Britain, and the first troops to go ashore were the 1st Battalions of the Hampshire Regiment and the Dorset Regiment. They leaped from their landing craft at 7.25am into 60cm (2ft) of water and waded the short distance to the beach. All the British landings, including JUNO and SWORD, were to be preceded by specialized armour, as Montgomery had planned. The employment of Hobart's 'funnies' undoubtedly made it much easier for the infantry to get ashore. The 'flail' tanks, in particular, proved a godsend in smashing paths through the coastal minefields, an asset the Americans unfortunately did not possess. The 1st Dorsets got ashore with remarkably little difficulty, due almost entirely to the operation of the 'funnies'. Within an hour armoured assault teams had cleared exits through the beaches and the battalion began to move inland with armoured support.

The Hampshires, however, had a much harder task. They landed close to Le Hamel on the western end of GOLD. Here the

LANDING: 7.25 AM

HOBART'S 'FUNNIES'

LE HAMEL

Germans had a major stronghold which Allied bombing and the naval bombardment had failed to destroy. The fire from Le Hamel was deadly and casualties mounted. Another OMAHA situation seemed in the making. But eventually the British infantry worked their way around the rear of the German position. Even so, Le Hamel was not finally taken until well into the afternoon of D-Day. By evening the British had taken the small port of **ARROMANCHES**, driving the Germans from the concrete fortifications on the cliffs overlooking the harbour. Arromanches was a vital objective, as it was here that, according to plans, the British MULBERRY B prefabricated harbour was due to be sited.

The 69th Brigade, consisting of the 6th and 7th Battalions of the Green Howards and the 5th Battalion of the East Yorkshire Regiment, went ashore on the eastern sector of GOLD beach close to **LA RIVIERE**. There was bitter street fighting among the ruins of the village, where a German 88-mm gun, firing from within a concrete pillbox, had earlier pinned the troops behind the sea wall. Again, British specialized armour saved the situation when a 'flail' tank destroyed the gun by getting in close and firing a shell through the narrow slit of the pillbox. The two follow-up brigades landed shortly before noon – an hour later than planned. The 151st, comprising three battalions of the Durham Light Infantry, struck southwest towards the Caen-Bayeux road, with the 56th Brigade (2nd Battalions Essex and Gloucestershire Regiments and the South Wales Borderers) on their right flank. By evening the whole spearhead division of British XXX Corps was ashore and moving rapidly towards **BAYEUX**. This historic town, with its famous Bayeux Tapestry, fell the next day – the first French town to be liberated by the Allies.

Meanwhile a force of the 47th Royal Marine Commandos bypassed Arromanches and was pushing westwards with the aim of capturing Port-en-Bessin and linking up with the Americans. The 47th, however, suffered badly during the landing. Of their 16 landing craft, 4 were destroyed by obstacles and 11 either damaged or beached. Their radios and heavy weapons were all lost as a result. Most of the men were obliged to swim ashore under constant heavy machine gun fire from the Germans. One Royal Marine is reported as having called out jokingly to his comrades: 'Perhaps we're intruding. This seems to be a private beach.' Despite the hot welcome that was given to them, the commandos suffered surprisingly few casualties.

French villagers around **ST COME-DE-FRESNES**, where the 47th Royal Marine commandos landed, could not believe it when they saw the British troops coming ashore from the hundreds of ships that lay off the coast. The sight was at first impossible for them to take in. Their joy and excitement knew no bounds in spite of the terrifying bombardment. Soon the bell of the little church of St Côme was pealing wildly to signal that their long dreamed of liberation from Nazi tyranny was here at last.

JUNO

JUNO beach was the target for the 3rd Canadian Division, led by Major General R.F.L. Keller supported by the 2nd Canadian Armoured Brigade. On D-Day the division formed part of British I Corps under the command of Lieutenant General J.T. Crocker. JUNO turned out to be the bloodiest of the three British beaches. It was strongly fortified and the existence of rocky reefs, many of them below the water line, made it more difficult to attack. German underwater obstacles caused havoc to the assault craft and many boats were either holed or blown up by mines. Groups of British Royal Marine frogmen went in with the Canadians to try to clear the underwater obstacles, having been well briefed in advance about what they were likely to find. These men performed miracles in helping to get the Canadian troops ashore.

Owing to the rough weather and the surging tide, the Canadians landed later than planned, coming ashore at about 7.35am. The 7th Brigade, made up of the Royal Winnipeg Rifles, the Regina Rifles and the Canadian Scottish, landed on the western edge of Courseulles assisted by DD tanks and 'flails'. Unfortunately, quite a lot of the specialized armour was delayed and the troops had to storm the beach without the protection they had been promised. The Canadian Division, which had not been in battle before, carried out the initial assault with great dash and spirit, but soon the devastating German fire from the shore defences began to take its toll. Casualties mounted rapidly, men being mowed down like corn as they raced across the exposed beach.

On the eastern sector of JUNO, where the 8th Brigade went in, the situation was even worse. Here there was practically no armoured support, as the seas were too rough for the DD tanks to be launched. At Bernières the men of the Queen's Own Rifles were carried onto the shore almost directly in front

Right: British DD amphibious tanks with infantry in support push inland from SWORD beach.

of a major German strongpoint. The battalion suffered heavy casualties trying to reach the cover of the sea wall, but a rocket-firing ship moved in close to the shore and poured concentrated fire upon the strongpoint which the Canadians then stormed and captured. By 9.30am Bernières had been cleared of the enemy, and the French Canadians of the Regiment de la Chaudière, following up, were already moving through the little resort to push south towards Bény-sur-Mer which lay 5 km (3 miles) inland.

Meanwhile, bitter fighting was taking place in the gardens and narrow streets of Courseulles. The battle to clear the Germans out of the tiny town lasted well into the afternoon of D-Day. Congestion along the beaches both here and at Bernières delayed any chance to break free of the coastal strip. Armour, vehicles and fresh troops began to crowd together on the shoreline while wrecked tanks and landing craft were strewn along the water's edge.

As they moved inland, the Canadian infantry became the target for concentrated fire from German machine guns and 88-mm artillery, but they pushed on steadily, destroying batteries and taking a considerable

COURSEULLES

Left: Vivent les Anglais! A smiling Frenchwoman greets the Green Howards of British XXX Corps as they enter the village of St Gabriel near Creully on 7 June 1944. These troops landed on GOLD beach.

number of prisoners. In spite of the heavy losses sustained during the landing, the Canadian 3rd Division staged a brilliant recovery. It advanced further on D-Day than any other Allied formation. By nightfall the division had pushed about 13 km (8 miles) inland, while Canadian armoured patrols had got as far as the main road between Caen and Bayeux, 16 km (10 miles) from the beach. Fierce German resistance as they neared Caen prevented them from fully exploiting their advance. Even so, the Canadian performance on D-Day was unquestionably a success. They displayed great gallantry and determination and could justly claim to have avenged in full measure those of their comrades who had suffered so terribly during the disastrous raid at Dieppe nearly two years before.

SECTORS

The British landing beaches, like the American ones, had been subdivided into sectors using the alphabetical code of the day. On GOLD the sectors, running from west to east, were code-named Item, Jig and King. JUNO's beaches were similarly Love, Mike and Nan, while SWORD beach was quartered into Oboe, Peter, Queen and Roger. Although JUNO was predominantly a Canadian beach on D-Day, British troops also came ashore there. Part of the 4th British Special Services Brigade, which included No. 48 Royal Marine Commando, landed on JUNO's Nan sector east of Bernières at 9am on D-Day. All six of their landing craft were damaged on the run-in to the beach and a number of men drowned. Those who reached the beach came under murderous fire from German gun emplacements in St Aubin. The 48th Commandos had the important task of fighting their way eastwards to join up with the British landing on SWORD, but they quickly ran into strong German positions around Langrune-sur-Mer. Mines, barbed wire and concrete barriers made it impossible for the commandos, who were without artillery or tanks, to break through. Langrune proved a tough nut to crack and German

LANGRUNE-SUR-MER

resistance there was not overcome until the following day.

SWORD

SWORD beach, like JUNO, was the responsibility of Crocker's British I Corps. The assault troops in this case were from the 3rd British Infantry Division, under the temporary command of Major General T.G. Rennie. Although SWORD beach contained four sectors, almost all the landings on D-Day were carried out in just one sector, Queen, which extended for a little over 1.5 km (1 mile) between Lion-sur-Mer and the western edge of Ouistreham. The attack was thus concentrated on a narrow one-brigade front.

For once the DD tanks and other armour came in exactly on time and ahead of the infantry. The 8th Brigade, with the 1st Battalion of the South Lancashire Regiment on the right and the 2nd East Yorkshire on the

Above: British 105-mm self-propelled guns in action in a Normandy field inland from SWORD beach on D-Day.

LANDING: 7.25 AM

left, stormed ashore at 7.25am. By comparison with the other Allied beaches, this part of the coast was an almost entirely built-up area, with houses stretching all the way along the coast road immediately behind the dunes. After getting ashore with minimum casualties, the 8th Brigade attacked the powerful German strongpoint at La Brèche on the edge of Lion-sur-Mer and started to mop up the German snipers and machine-gun nests entrenched in the coastal villas. Exits for the armour were quickly established and the South Lancashire Battalion moved inland to capture Hermanville by 10am. The East Yorkshire Battalion on the other flank, however, had a much more difficult time. Mortar

fire and machine guns caused heavy casualties among the first wave to hit the beach, and the follow-up troops reported having to pass through piles of dead and wounded. The 1st Special Services Brigade (Commandos), led by Brigadier the Lord Lovat, also landed on the eastern edge of SWORD and pushed eastwards into the streets of Ouistreham. While some of the commandos, including a Free French detachment, fought their way into the strongly fortified town, the rest of the force, wearing their distinctive green berets instead of steel helmets, struck inland to join up with the British 6th Airborne, who were clinging to the Orne bridges under repeated German counterattacks. At 1.30pm Gale's paratroops, waiting anxiously for reinforcements, heard to their delight the stirring sound of the bagpipes and saw the jaunty Lovat, preceded by his piper, striding at the head of his men towards the Bénouville canal bridge. For the tired men of the 6th Airborne, who had been fighting nonstop for twelve hours, it was a moment to savour.

It was in the SWORD sector on the afternoon of D-Day that the feared German armour made its first appearance. The 21st Panzer Division, positioned on the southeast edge of Caen, was ordered up to attack the British bridgehead. Its tanks moved north on the west bank of the River Orne, where they were engaged by antitank guns of the 1st Battalion of the King's Shropshire Light Infantry and three tank squadrons of the Staffordshire Yeomanry. The British force, which was on well-chosen ground on the top of Périers Ridge 5 km (3 miles) from the coast, opened fire with great accuracy. Sixteen German tanks were destroyed and the panzer attack was thrown back. But about 1.5 km (1 mile) to the west another group from the same

division, mostly mechanized infantry, pushed through the narrow gap between the British and Canadians and reached the sea near Luc-sur-Mer, where German troops were still holding out. The German penetration at this point could have been serious, but late in the evening the sky over the coast became filled with aircraft, as the 6th Airborne Division's remaining air-landing brigade was flown in. The sight of hundreds of gliders swooping down and crash-landing on both sides of the Orne so astonished the Germans that the 21st Panzer pulled back in some disarray.

The appearance of the panzer force had, however, put a stop to the somewhat ambitious British plan of seizing Caen on that first day. The Shropshires and the tanks of the Staffordshire Yeomanry got as far as Biéville, 6 km (3.5 miles) from Caen, when they were halted by German self-propelled guns and tanks and forced to withdraw. The chance to capture Caen quickly had vanished. What lay ahead was a bloody battle of attrition, which would last for weeks and, tragically, would reduce this ancient Norman cathedral town to a heap of rubble.

Above: British troops of the 4th Special Services Brigade taking cover from snipers in the ruined streets of St Aubin-sur-Mer. The German defenders had piled up tree trunks to form obstacles against the Allies' tanks.

Left: A long line of German prisoners being marched away by British troops after the landings.

The German Dilemma

Right: A German
defender's view of
the Allied invasion
fleet standing off the
Normandy coast on
D-Day.

THE WEATHER

The Allied invasion took the Germans completely by surprise. To a large extent this was due to the weather. Having seen no sign of an invasion attempt during May, when the weather was almost perfect, the Germans, not surprisingly, concluded that the Allies would never dare to risk a crossing while the weather in the Channel was stormy. So confident was the German High Command that there was no danger during the second week of June that a number of senior commanders had been invited to Rennes, in Brittany, to attend a war-games exercise and Field Marshal Rommel, Army Group B's commander-in-chief, had taken time off to visit his wife in Germany.

The absence of so many key figures played a major part in the slowness and lack of decision that characterized the German response. As the reports of parachute landings in the Cotentin and around the Orne began to come in during the early hours of 6 June, the German commanders on the spot were baffled. Was this the invasion or was it merely a diversionary raid? Looking back, it seems extraordinary that the Germans should imagine that the Allies would risk the lives of so many highly trained paratroops for a mere

UNCERTAINTY

diversionary operation. The truth was that the Germans were in many ways the victims of their own logic. To the German mind no one in his senses would willingly face the hazards of a long-range invasion of Normandy when he could take the easy route and attack across the 35 km (22 miles) that separated England from Calais. That, after all, had been the German plan for an invasion of England in 1940; it seemed only reasonable to assume that that would be the Allied plan for an invasion in reverse. What the Germans failed to realize was that the Allies, unlike the Germans in 1940, had total command of the sea as well as purpose-built landing craft. Even more important, they had total command of the air. Their range of invasion options was therefore much greater than that of the Germans four years earlier.

On the evening of 5 June the BBC, in its French Service, broadcast the long-awaited coded message to the French Resistance that an Allied invasion was imminent – that is, within 48 hours. As it happened, German Intelligence also knew the significance of this message and a warning was sent at once to Field Marshal von Rundstedt's headquarters in Paris. Amazingly, only the German 15th Army, guarding the Pas-de-Calais region of the coast, was put on alert. The 7th Army, in position along the Normandy coast, received no warning at all!

Rommel's Chief of Staff, General Hans Speidel, was completely at a loss. As reports of the first seaborne landings reached him after 7.30am, he still could not make up his mind whether or not this was a diversionary attack. But he did recognize that the scale of the assault was significant. He telephoned Rommel at 10.15am to report what was happening. Rommel was appalled and clearly badly shaken by the news. He immediately appreciated that this *was* the awaited invasion and that he, like the rest of the High Command, had been caught napping. 'How

stupid of me', he kept repeating, and at once hurried back to Normandy to take charge of the critical situation.

Meanwhile, the Commander-in-Chief West, Field Marshal von Rundstedt, had acted on his own initiative by ordering the two reserve panzer divisions stationed west of Paris to move to the Normandy coast. However, he later learned to his disgust that General Jodl at Hitler's Berchtesgaden headquarters had countermanded the order. The panzer reserves could not be moved without Hitler's express permission. He was asleep in bed and no-one dared to wake him. What is

Right: German motorized infantry calmly await the order to launch a counterattack against the encroaching Allied bridgehead.

ROMMEL

VON RUNDSTEDT

more, even when Hitler was finally informed of the Allied landings, he agreed that no action need be taken until the Allied intentions became clear. This delay was crucial. By the afternoon of D-Day still no decision had been taken to commit the reserves and the staff at Rommel's headquarters were nearly frantic. At last a message was received from Hitler agreeing to release the two additional panzer divisions, the 12th SS Panzer and Panzer Lehr, but still insisting that the troops and armour of the powerful 15th Army defending Calais were not to be moved. Further appeals to Hitler from von Rundstedt to be allowed to commit all the reserves fell on deaf ears. As a result the 19 divisions in the Calais region remained where they were, facing out to sea waiting for a second invasion that would never come.

CRUCIAL DELAY

The British deception plan had succeeded beyond the Allies' wildest dreams. German Intelligence had been completely fooled into

BRITISH DECEPTION

seriously overestimating the size of the Allied forces in Britain. A report submitted to Hitler at midday on D-Day made clear the extent of the Germans' miscalculation: 'Not a single unit of the 1st US Army Group located north and south of the Thames has so far been committed. The same is true of the 10 to 12 formations stationed in central England and in Scotland.' The report concluded that this could only suggest a further large-scale operation in the Channel, which one must expect to be made against the Pas-de-Calais. The fictitious armies dreamed up by FORTITUDE thus played a vital part in keeping the Germans guessing and undoubtedly helped to delay a full-scale counterattack, which might have pushed the Allied assault troops back into the sea, forestalling liberation.

The deception was prolonged by broadcast messages on D-Day to the peoples of Occupied Europe. The Belgian Prime Minister, Hubert Pierlot, told his compatriots that

Right: Hitler's brief crisis meeting with Rommel and other senior Army commanders at Margival near Paris, 17 June 1944. This was the last time that the *Führer* set foot on French soil.

D-DAY BROADCASTS

Left: German '*nebelwerfer*' rocket launchers in a prepared defensive position near Caen. The '*nebelwerfer*' was known to Allied troops as 'Moaning Minnie'.

further landings along the coast of Belgium might be imminent, while Norway's King Haakon, in exile in London, told his countrymen that the Normandy landings were only an initial assault. Winston Churchill, too, suggested that further surprises to the enemy were forthcoming.

But, deception measures aside, what really prevented the Germans from gauging the scale and location of the invasion was the failure of the *Luftwaffe* to operate over the Channel area. Without the intelligence provided by aerial reconnaissance the German High Command was operating in the dark. The initial Allied victory on the Normandy beaches was thus largely made possible by a combination of brilliant deception strategy and overwhelming air superiority. By the time the Germans reacted it was already too late.

ABSENCE OF THE LUFTWAFFE

CHAPTER SIXTEEN

The Allied Bridgehead

Right: The Allied build-up in the Normandy bridgehead gets under way. Despite the chaos on OMAHA beach on D-Day, the Americans rapidly restored order and vehicles and supplies were soon streaming ashore.

THE NEWS IS OUT

The first official news of the Allied landings was flashed to the world at around 9.30am (British time) on D-Day. The BBC's well-known newsreader John Snagge had the privilege of making the historic announcement:

> This is London, London calling in the Home, Overseas and European Services of the BBC and through United Nations Radio Mediterranean. And this is John Snagge speaking. Under the command of General Eisenhower Allied naval forces supported by strong air forces began landing Allied armies this morning on the northern coasts of France . . .

The whole of Britain was electrified by the news. In homes and factories, even in schools, the word spread like wildfire and millions gathered around their radios to wait for further details. On the other side of the Atlantic Americans woke up to learn that the long-awaited assault on the European continent had begun. Banner headlines bearing the word 'INVASION' were splashed across the early editions of the East Coast newspapers and all over the United States, as D-Day 6 June dawned, there was a wave of excitement and expectancy. In the streets of New York people prayed openly for the success of the

Right: OMAHA, D+3. Trucks, bulldozers and jeeps assist in clearing the beach after the initial assault so that reinforcementts can be landed. American signals troops have already set up telephone poles to provide the vital communications links with forward positions.

On June 4 Portsmouth Dockyard was alive with military vehicles of every description, tanks, armoured cars and trucks . . . When we set sail, landing craft were everywhere, filled with soldiers, their faces blackened ready for combat.

We anchored with the rest of the great armada off the Isle of Wight and then learned that the invasion was postponed for 24 hours because of rough weather.

The evening of June 5 came, the seas were still very rough. But, the invasion was on despite the rough seas.

We were taking part at dawn the next day, June 6, in the D-Day landings, three weeks after my 18th birthday.

The invasion began at 6.30am. Our target was the town of Ouistreham. Our instructions were to bombard the town with our main guns, to soften up the German garrison. On our way across, we all had to make a will. The Captain spoke to us over the address system telling us that they didn't know what to expect from the German defence and 'that by this time tomorrow we could all be in Kingdom Come'.

. . . When we arrived off Normandy the bombardment began. It was like all Hell had been let loose. Ships of all the Allied navies, large and small, were shelling the coast. The noise was incredible. The sky was full of aircraft towing gliders filled with paratroopers that would be landing in enemy occupied territory. As we fired salvo after salvo our ship vibrated to the extent that everything had to be battened down. The air was filled with cordite fumes. Orders were barked down voice pipes from the bridge as we went about our tasks like clockwork.

As the day wore on we were allowed to return to the mess-deck, two men at a time, for a drink of cocoa and a sandwich. Whilst I was in the mess-deck I heard a violent explosion. All the men not on watch were ordered to the port side. A ship had been sunk and survivors were in the water. We threw a scrambling net over the side and our ship stopped to allow them to climb aboard. The men were covered in oil, some wounded, others obviously stunned. We reached down to haul them aboard, the deck was a mixture of water, oil and blood. . .

Wilfred Foulds, RN on the Cruiser HMS *Scylla*. This Cruiser was the flagship of Rear Admiral Vian who commanded the Eastern Task Force on D-Day.

Allied armies. Everywhere there was a sense of great emotion.

The first terse communiqué issued by General Eisenhower's Supreme Allied Headquarters in Southwick House had been careful to omit any reference to the actual locations of the landings, but German radio broadcasts had already spoken of landings on the southern side of the Bay of the Seine from Cherbourg to Le Havre. By midday on D-Day it had become clear that the area of the main landings was Normandy. 'WE WIN BEACH-HEADS' announced the London *Evening News*, adding reassuringly that everything was 'going according to plan'. Meanwhile, the BBC, whose role as an Allied propaganda weapon had been considerable, broadcast Eisenhower's message to the peoples of Nazi-occupied Europe:

Although the initial assault may not have been made in your own country, the hour of your liberation is approaching. All patriots, men and women, young and old, have a part to play in the achievement of final victory . . . Wait until I give you the signal to rise and strike the enemy.

THE GERMAN VIEW

The German propaganda machine had quickly swung into action. Conceding that the Allies had launched a surprise attack, German radio sought to reassure its listeners that no breakthrough of the Atlantic Wall had taken place. The German forces, it insisted, were more than capable of defeating the Allied invaders, who would soon be thrown back into the sea.

D+1: 7 JUNE

By the morning of D + 1 (7 June) the shape of the Allied foothold on the Normandy coast had become clear. It had not yet coalesced into a single bridgehead; instead it resembled four separate chunks. The biggest areas held were on the British beaches, where British XXX Corps on GOLD and the Canadians of British I Corps on JUNO together formed a single wedge 18 km (11 miles) long by 11 km (7 miles) deep. However, the British troops on

SWORD and the 6th Airborne Division east of the Orne were still not linked up with the Canadians on their right flank. Similarly, the Americans of Gerow's 5th Corps on OMAHA, clinging to a narrow toehold, were isolated both from the British on their left and from Collins' US 7th Corps on the western side of the Vire estuary.

The size of the Allied foothold was much smaller than Eisenhower and Montgomery had intended. The Americans were well short of their D-Day target lines. Above all, the British had notably failed to capture Caen which for Montgomery had been the major D-Day objective. Nevertheless, the Allies had every reason to be satisfied. They had

Right: An American Sherman tank is guided down the ramp of a British-crewed landing ship onto OMAHA beach.

Left: French civilians
flee the centre of Pont
l'Abbé in the Cotentin
peninsula to escape
the fierce fighting.
Wrecked German
vehicles and corpses
litter the street.

Below: A British
soldier of the Durham
Light Infantry,
wounded in the
heavy fighting near
Tilly-sur-Seulles, is
given a cigarette at a
Regimental Aid Post.

smashed their way into Hitler's Fortress Europe along a 50 km (30 mile) length of coast and had overwhelmed the formidable shore defences. This they had accomplished at a total cost of around 10,000 casualties, of which around 3,600 were British and Canadian and about 6,000 American – a far lower casualty rate than anyone among the Allied command had dared anticipate.

CASUALTIES

By midnight on D-Day the Allies had succeeded in landing more than 130,000 men, of whom 75,000 were put ashore on the British beaches and around 57,000 on UTAH and OMAHA. In addition, nearly 16,000 American and about 7,500 British airborne troops had been dropped or landed. It was a quite magnificent achievement without parallel in the history of war. Perhaps no-one realized this better than the Soviet leader, Marshal Stalin, whose armies stood to benefit most from the consequences of the British-American assault. In a telegraphed message to

**THE ALLIED
ACHIEVEMENT**

STALIN'S TRIBUTE

Churchill, Stalin paid this generous tribute to the participating Allied forces:

> My colleagues and I cannot but admit that the history of warfare knows no like undertaking from the point of view of its scale, its vast conception and its masterly execution. Napoleon in his time failed ignominiously to force the Channel. Only our allies have succeeded in realizing with honour the grandiose plan. History will record this deed as an achievement of the highest order.

In spite of their initial success in getting their armies ashore, the Allies knew that the bridgeheads were anything but secure. General Montgomery, the overall land commander, set up his advanced operational headquarters in the château of Creully, 7 km (4 miles) inland from GOLD beach. At dawn on 7 June he held a conference with General Bradley, commander of the US 1st Army, and General Sir Miles Dempsey, commander of the British 2nd. The commanders knew that they faced grave problems. The room for manoeuvre that Montgomery considered essential had not yet been achieved and there was an urgent need to expand and unite the bridgeheads. The first priority, therefore, was to thrust inland, gain territory and build up Allied strength in time to meet the inevitable German counterattack.

That counterattack was already being set in motion. Four battle-hardened panzer divisions, Panzer Lehr, the 2nd and 12th SS and the 17th Panzer Grenadier, were on their way to the Normandy coast, while two further panzer divisions were being recalled from the Russian front. Other infantry divisions were being hastily moved eastwards from Brittany. Shortly after D-Day the Germans stumbled upon an important piece of intelligence.

ALLIED CONFERENCE

GERMAN COUNTERATTACK

Documents recovered from the bodies of two dead American officers turned out to be the operational orders for both the US corps that had already landed. The information was at once handed over to German 7th Army headquarters at Le Mans, where it was soon recognized that the American operation was a big one. From this the Germans correctly deduced that the Normandy assault was indeed the main invasion and that there was little likelihood now of a second landing around Calais. Von Rundstedt thereupon repeated his request to Hitler for all reserves to be committed, and this time he got them. For the Allies, therefore, it would be a race against time.

Above: The Allied Army commanders meeting for the first time on French soil. Left to right: General Omar Bradley, US 1st Army; General Sir Bernard Montgomery, C in C Allied Land Forces; General Sir Miles Dempsey, British 2nd Army.

CHAPTER SEVENTEEN

MULBERRY – An Engineering Miracle

For the Allies the most important requirement after D-Day was the capture of a port. Only with safe and reliable dock facilities could they land the supplies their armies needed. Cherbourg was, of course, the primary objective, but in the meantime they would have to rely on other means. For months the British had been hard at work constructing and fitting two huge prefabricated harbours, the so-called MULBERRIES, together able to provide port facilities equal in size to the British port of Dover. And on 7 June the first of the MULBERRY components was towed across the Channel. One harbour, MULBERRY A, was to be installed off OMAHA beach to supply the Americans; the second, MULBERRY B, was to be sited off Arromanches to supply the British.

The artificial harbours were a monument to Allied ingenuity and purpose. They were complex engineering structures of unprecedented weight and size, each being the height of a tall building. To move them would require a sizable fleet of tugs. Once across the Channel, they would be sunk in place. In addition, the MULBERRIES were to be provided with their own breakwaters, which would take the form of old British ships, some of them warships, loaded with sand ballast and sunk onto the seabed. Besides these massive outer breakwaters, code-named GOOSEBERRIES, there were nearly 150 concrete caissons, known as PHOENIXES, which would provide the inner breakwaters and serve as supports for the main MULBERRY structures. Each completed harbour would

also have four floating piers running from the pierheads to the beaches. Transport and landing ships would be able to unload at the pierheads straight into trucks, while large Liberty ships and other big vessels could discharge their cargoes into barges.

Ultimately, the success of the Allied invasion would depend upon these transportable harbours, which, once in position, would be able to handle up to 12,000 tonnes (tons) of supplies daily. But the Allies were well aware that they were extremely vulnerable to air attack. They could not be camouflaged and their movement across the Channel was a constant worry to Eisenhower and the Allied team. Towing them also set a major problem. In the end every available tugboat in Britain and along the Atlantic coast of the United States had to be brought in to do the momentous job.

MULBERRY A was put into position first. As the task force, much of it crewed by merchant navy volunteers, moved in towards the coast it came under heavy fire from German long-range guns. One by one the ships manoeuvred close inshore to be sunk in their assigned positions. As ship after ship exploded and settled in the water most of the American troops watching from the shore assumed that they had been sunk by gunfire. So did the Germans. When the largest of the old warships, the 25,000-tonne (ton) HMS *Centurion*, went to the bottom, the Germans were jubilant. That same night German radio announced that a major British warship had been sunk off the Normandy coast with huge

MULBERRY A

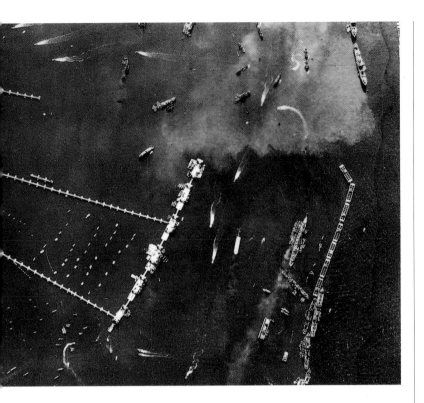

MULBERRY B

loss of life. In reality the ship had been deliberately sunk by charges placed in the hull and the crew of 70 British sailors had been safely taken off beforehand.

A team of American Seabees under the command of Captain Augustus Clark of the US Navy worked flat out to get MULBERRY A put together. Clark was a hard taskmaster and his drive and determination helped to ensure that the American harbour was in partial operation less than a week after D-Day, although it was not – and, tragically, never would be – completed. MULBERRY B in the British sector was assembled rather more slowly, but, as events proved, it would endure and eventually play a crucial role in getting the Allied follow-up formations ashore.

The MULBERRY harbours remain one of the legendary achievements of the Allied invasion of Normandy. This gigantic enterprise was yet another example of the extensive planning and close cooperation which went into the Anglo-American effort.

As an army driver I recall that first week in June 1944 so well. There were flags and bunting all the way, with cheering crowds yelling 'Good luck, Boys!' and giving us cups of tea to help us along.

Once at London Docks we were sealed off from the outside world. No letters, no phoning, for we had now been officially told our destination was France. Work consisted of waterproofing vehicles and checking equipment. Once aboard, we rendezvoused with a Naval Escort and put our vomiting bags to good use. I wrote to my mother: 'Here I am en route to Normandy by courtesy of the Royal Navy – Not a Jerry plane in sight, the RAF rules the skies.'

Luckily our landing was dry. I clearly remember driving across the beach between white ribbons – the sign that it had been cleared of land mines. The few houses were just ruins. British bombers had gone in before us, the Germans had retreated and the fighting was going on way ahead of us. But British troops and vehicles were everywhere. We headed a few miles inland to a deserted farm house. Our first task was to unload the camouflage nets and remove sticky waterproofing from our hot engines, and then to dig in. That first night we were ordered to sleep under our lorries but I found a stretcher and had a comfortable night's sleep in the back of mine . . .

The most memorable thing about that first day in France was the smell: the stench of death. Not human flesh, but cattle. Scores of them all lying on their sides – pot bellied and dead. The sun didn't help much.

. . . The organization and planning of the D-Day operation was brilliant – absolutely nothing was forgotten . . . On landing, each man was given a preprinted Field Postcard on which to write home. It consisted of sentences such as 'I am well' or 'I have been wounded' which could be struck out. We all had tin rations plus a portable cooker with tiny solid fuel tablets. I can still recall the delicious steak and kidney puddings . . . Special praise, too for the Army Laundry Ablution Units. Dirty shirts and underwear were just exchanged for clean ones, and if they fitted you were lucky! Every day was an uncertain one, but the comradeship and spirit has never been equalled.

John Frost

Left: An aerial view of the British MULBERRY harbour at Arromanches. This artificial port provided sheltered landing facilities for both landing craft and large merchant ships. The sunken blockships and caissons form an outer breakwater, while the long piers radiate outwards from the shore.

Build Up

Immediately after D-Day the Allied forces began to push steadily forward in an effort to widen the narrow bridgehead. On 8 June the British and Americans succeeded in linking up at Port-en-Bessin, the small harbour northwest of Bayeux that was to mark the dividing line between the two armies. Three days later, on 11 June, the 101st Airborne Division captured the important town of Carentan after bitter fighting along the causeways that led across the flooded areas. The following day the 101st was able to join up with the US 5th Corps fighting its way westwards from OMAHA. The British and

Canadians in the meantime had closed the gap between them north of Caen so that a single Allied front was now established. It ran from north of Ste Mère-Eglise in the Cotentin to Ranville just east of the Orne.

In spite of their shattering ordeal on D-Day, the Americans on OMAHA recovered with remarkable speed. Order was rapidly restored along the beach and soon additional supplies and troops were pouring ashore. The 2nd Infantry Division joined the 1st and 29th Divisions and pushed ahead at such a pace that very soon the American forces had outstripped the British on their left and had

**8 JUNE:
PORT-EN-BESSIN**

11 JUNE: CARENTAN

**A SINGLE ALLIED
FRONT**

penetrated 25 km (15 miles) inland, threatening both Caumont and the key regional centre of St Lô in the Vire valley.

RESISTANCE HARDENS

The British and Canadians meanwhile were coming up against solid German opposition. After their initial dash on D-Day they were making little headway. From the start Rommel had assessed that the British penetration constituted the main danger. He was concerned in particular with the threat posed by the 6th Airborne Division east of the Orne, fearing that it could lead to an Allied break out towards Paris and the Seine. By 8 June the Germans had begun to concentrate their panzer strength against the British front and quickly established a strong defence line with artillery and tanks on the northern outskirts of Caen. Several bloody tank skirmishes took place, especially between the Canadians and the newly arrived 12th SS Panzer Division. This division, known as the Hitler Jugend, was composed of fanatical young Nazi troops led by an experienced tank commander, Kurt Meyer, who was revered by his men. They were tough, highly trained and immensely self-confident. Soon they became locked in a savage vendetta with the Canadians, murdering some Canadian prisoners in cold blood.

HITLER JUGEND

Left: A Canadian Army Chaplain helps tend a soldier wounded in the fighting near Caen.

Right: The Odon
offensive. Troops of
the 15th Scottish
Division advance
with bayonets fixed
across a wheatfield
to engage the enemy.

The Crossing (5–6 June 1944)

They nestle round the ports and shores of England's
south,
The many thousand craft that lie in wait –
All filling with the arms of war, and buoyant youth –
Preparing to sail, shortly, to their fate.

When from our commanders, for this crusade ahead,
The signal comes – 'Proceed to France!' is clear.
It's said that 'gentlemen in England now a-bed
Should think themselves accurs'd they were not here'.

Ah, what a worthy ship, our sleek destroyer *Scourge*,
That bears us on, ahead of this huge thrust –
Our pride too great to hide, the moment we emerge
As escort for the brave minesweepers' trust.

The decks are cleared by all, but those who work below,
While we pass through the minefield's moonlight gleam;
And at three knots, a speed so tantalizing – slow –
We watch the loose mines, bobbing by our beam.

The gliders and their tugs are passing overhead –
They're sure to have a special part to play,
And from the ships below some silent prayers are said,
For those who'll be the first to France this way.

Our *Svenner*, sister ship, at early dawn is lost –
Torpedoed – in the E-boats only raid –
Alas, the first of this vast fleet to pay the cost,
As Norway's mark on OVERLORD is made.

We meet the midget sub', at SWORD's most eastern
coast –
Relieve her, and take on her guiding role;
But soon we're called again – 'Take up bombarding
post!' –
A German gun emplacement is our goal.

James Hinton

Recognizing that Caen could not now easily be taken by direct frontal attack, Montgomery decided to try an outflanking move. His plan was to move the newly landed British 7th Armoured Division through the edge of the American-held sector north of Caumont and swing it eastwards in a right hook towards the town of Villers-Bocage. The British thrust was, however, to end in a humiliating failure.

The 7th Armoured was potentially one of Montgomery's best divisions. It had fought with distinction against Rommel in North Africa, earning the troops the now famous nickname 'Desert Rats'. Unfortunately, on being brought back to Britain from Italy in readiness for the invasion, the division had been forced to leave behind virtually all its Sherman tanks, guns and other weapons. Instead, it had been fitted out with British light-medium Cromwell tanks and even with Honeys, which were also light tanks and quite obsolete. Its equipment, in other words, was completely unsuitable for taking on the much superior and more heavily armoured German tanks such as the Mark IVs and powerful Mark V Panthers.

On 13 June, one week after D-Day, the 7th Armoured sent its advanced formations into Villers-Bocage. They had no sooner passed

**7TH ARMOURED
DIVISION**

**13 JUNE:
VILLERS-BOCAGE**

A LONE TIGER

Below: British
infantry crouched in
an orchard await the
order to advance.

into the countryside east of the town than they were ambushed by a squadron of heavy Tiger tanks belonging to General Bayerlein's Panzer Lehr – probably the best of Rommel's panzer divisions. What took place has become legend. One lone Tiger, commanded by Obersturmführer Michael Wittmann, a German tank ace who had won a reputation on the Russian front, opened fire from the cover of a wood. The first shell from Wittman's 88-mm gun smashed into the leading personnel carrier, setting it ablaze. The Tiger then emerged from cover and within the space of a few minutes destroyed 25 armoured vehicles, both tanks and half tracks. The British tank crews, firing in reply, were horrified to find the shells from their own 75-mm guns bouncing off the giant Tiger's armour as if they were pellets from a toy gun. The encounter shocked the Desert Rats. And that was only the beginning. Other Tigers then appeared, inflicting further losses on the British formation, which retreated to Villers-Bocage. The German division, with strong infantry support, then launched a counterattack and retook the town. The 7th Armoured was finally pulled back 6.5km (4 miles)towards Caumont, having suffered heavy losses in both

WITHDRAWAL OF 7TH
ARMOURED

SUPERIORITY OF
GERMAN ARMOUR

Below: Guns of the 64th Regiment, Royal Artillery firing in support of British infantry near Tilly-sur-Seulles. The accuracy and intensity of British artillery fire was a constant worry to the Germans throughout the Normandy campaign.

vehicles and men. British antitank guns, firing at point blank range, admittedly took some toll of the German armour, but Montgomery's attempt to outflank Caen had been decisively thwarted.

Throughout the Normandy fighting the Allies were often to find themselves at a disadvantage when they faced the German armour. Although their standard battle tank, the American Sherman, was faster and more manoeuvrable than the German tanks, it was regularly outgunned and its armour was not thick enough to withstand the deadly German 88s. Faced by a Tiger or by the still heavier Royal Tiger, the Sherman was almost helpless. It also tended to catch fire rather too easily. The rule among tank crews when dealing with a Tiger was to send four Shermans or four Churchills and expect to lose three of them. Failure to equip their forces with a battle tank that could engage the German heavy armour on equal terms was

one of the most costly weaknesses of the Allies' invasion planning. The horrific spectacle of tanks being set ablaze and their crews incinerated, a process which the troops cynically referred to as 'brewing up', became part of everyday experience on the Normandy battlefield.

As they pushed southwards from the coast, the Americans and British soon found themselves in the peculiar terrain for which Normandy is famous, the *bocage* country. *Bocage* literally means a copse or woodland, but in Normandy is the name given to describe the pattern of small fields and orchards bordered by stone walls and high hedges that dominate the landscape. The *bocage*, as the Allies discovered, is ideal ground for a defender, providing natural cover for snipers and tanks. It is crisscrossed by narrow sunken lanes, which are difficult for vehicles to negotiate. The hedges, set on high banks, are in places so thick that not even a tank can force a way through. This was the obstacle that the Allies began to come up against, and the Germans, defending with skill, used it to maximum advantage.

The British 7th Armoured Division had been withdrawn not merely because of the hammering it had received from Panzer Lehr, but also because of the unexpected appearance near Caumont of a new German armoured division, the 2nd Panzer, which had been secretly moved from Amiens, 130 km (80 miles) north of Paris. The British now had all four of the panzer divisions in Normandy ranged against them, which suited Montgomery, as his intention all along had been to draw the German armour onto the British front to allow the Americans to expand to the west. In this, some might argue, he had succeeded all too well. The British 2nd Army was soon engaged in a bitter slogging match right along the front from Caumont to the Orne, with a savage battle building up around the large village of Tilly-sur-Seulles.

Above: A British mine-clearing party of the 1st Dorsets moving cautiously through the streets of the bitterly contested village of Tilly-sur-Seulles after it had been captured on 20 June 1944.

The village, or what remained of it, was taken and retaken 23 times in the 10-day struggle that ended on 20 June, when the exhausted veterans of British XXX Corps finally ousted the fiercely resisting troops of Panzer Lehr.

Meanwhile, on the American front Bradley's initial drive to try to take St Lô had been repulsed with heavy losses. The Americans, like the British, were discovering the difficulties of adapting to the *bocage*, where every hedge, every cornfield, every clump of woodland had German troops and self-propelled guns concealed and waiting. Nevertheless, Rommel was increasingly worried about the threat developing further north in the Cotentin, where American strength near UTAH was building up to such a point that the German line could barely hold. Lawton Collins' 7th Corps had been reinforced by two more infantry divisions, the 90th and the 9th, which were pressing westwards hard in a bid to cut off the peninsula and so isolate Cherbourg.

The Germans, whose four divisions in the peninsula had received no reinforcements, were fiercely contesting every step. But Rommel dared not pull his troops out of the peninsula, as Hitler considered it imperative that the Allies be denied the use of the port and had given strict orders that Cherbourg was to be defended at all costs.

Hitler's order effectively sealed the fate of the German troops. Their line cracked around St Sauveur and the American 9th Division triumphantly reached the west coast at Barneville on 18 June, cutting off the base of the peninsula. Collins then regrouped his forces. The two airborne divisions, the 82nd and 101st, were positioned to hold his southern flank, which was partly protected by large flooded areas, while the 4th and 9th Divisions, joined by the newly landed 79th, prepared to strike north towards Cherbourg.

THE GREAT STORM

At the very moment when the Allied build up in the bridgehead was getting into its stride, disaster struck. On 19 June – which the superstitious were quick to point out was in fact D + 13 – a gale sprang up in the Channel which rapidly developed into a storm of some intensity. Experts said later that it was the worst summer storm to hit the English and French Channel coasts for more than 40 years. It lasted for more than three days and its effect upon Allied shipping and supply lines was little short of catastrophic. The storm wreaked its worst havoc upon the two MULBERRY harbours, which were still in the process of construction. As the wind and waves increased in ferocity, the huge concrete caissons began to drift and the harbours began to break up. Angry seas picked up landing ships and flung them against the breakwaters. The American MULBERRY A off OMAHA beach was eventually past all hope of repair. General Bradley wrote that when he

CHERBOURG ISOLATED

19 JUNE

DESTRUCTION OF MULBERRY A

Right: The port of
Cherbourg burning
after being set alight
by the Germans as
the Americans
entered the town.

Right: The port of Cherbourg burning after being set alight by the Germans as the Americans entered the town.

A HEAVY TOLL

and his staff went to inspect it on 22 June, he was appalled: the destruction was even worse than on D-Day. Wrecked vessels were scattered in confusion along the length of the beach. The storm damaged or destroyed 800 ships and landing craft along the invasion coast, four times as many as were lost on D-Day itself, and proved a cruel blow.

The British MULBERRY at Arromanches, although damaged, did not suffer as badly as the American harbour and was fairly quickly repaired. Even so, the reduction in Allied supplies was serious. Many convoys had had to turn back to port in England and for the three to four days the storm raged, little could be landed. As a result, Bradley's forces were starting to run dangerously short of ammunition, while Dempsey's 2nd Army was still lacking three divisions which by now should have been ashore. Eisenhower later wrote that the consequences of the great storm were so serious as to 'imperil our very foothold on the Continent'.

THE CAPTURE OF CHERBOURG

After the destruction caused by the storm the capture of the big French port of Cherbourg became increasingly urgent. Bradley ordered Collins to push ahead with all speed, and his subordinate needed no second bidding. Collins was by nature an aggressive general who liked to keep up constant pressure on the enemy. He had earlier commanded a division in Guadalcanal in the Pacific and, having learned to adapt to jungle conditions, quickly developed his own method for dealing with the *bocage*. Having taken Valognes, his three infantry divisions made rapid progress up the peninsula, and by 22 June American troops were fighting in the outskirts of Cherbourg itself. But the German garrison commanded by Lieutenant General Karl von Schlieben fought tenaciously, even though they knew that their position was hopeless and the defenders had to be blasted out of their concrete strongpoints one by one. The Americans finally called in the help of a British psychological warfare team, comprising an Intelligence Corps sergeant and a small Royal Signals unit, whose loudspeaker appeals successfully resulted in the surrender of several thousand Germans. American bombers gave support to the ground troops by attacking the port and fortifications, but the German battle group defending the port held on. Cherbourg is protected on the southern side by a high ridge of cliffs on which stands the Fort de Roule; the Germans had turned this into their main bastion. All attempts to take the fort were repulsed, but it finally fell to repeated

COLLINS

22 JUNE

FORT DU ROULE

and determined assaults by the 79th Division, attacking in the centre.

On 26 June von Schlieben at last surrendered and the American flag and the French tricolour were triumphantly hoisted over the town. Yet the German garrison had put up a truly stubborn defence. Several of the forts around the harbour continued to resist for a further two days, their beleaguered troops obeying to the last Hitler's order to deny the Allies the port.

The capture of Cherbourg was an important victory for the Allies. It was their biggest prize yet in the Normandy campaign. But the Germans had systematically destroyed the harbour installations and it would be many weeks before the port would be made operational. As June drew to its close the Allies had succeeded in getting as many as 26 divisions ashore, while the Germans facing them had around 20 divisions, most of them below strength. The build up was going in Montgomery's favour, even though the threat of German infantry divisions being moved from the 15th Army could not be discounted. At this point Montgomery decided the time had come to make a fresh attempt to encircle his principal objective – Caen.

Right: American infantry move forward along a hedge-bordered lane near Valognes during the advance on Cherbourg.

CHAPTER NINETEEN

The Battle for Caen

Right: German heavy Tiger tanks roll forward in a column preceded by a scout car. These feared 56-ton monsters proved more than a match for the Allied armour. Only some British Shermans fitted with a heavy 17-pounder gun were able to stand up to them.

20 JUNE: GERMAN PLAN

The Germans were preparing what they hoped would prove a decisive counter-thrust. At a conference on 20 June Hitler ordered Rommel to launch an attack with four panzer divisions near Caumont, at the point where the American and British armies joined. The panzers were to drive northwards until they reached the sea, thus splitting the Allied bridgehead in two. The timing was important: the offensive had to get under way before the American divisions attacking Cherbourg could be brought back to strengthen the southern front.

The Germans, however, had a problem in that they lacked sufficient infantry reserves to back up the armour. Hitler had gone back on his earlier promise to commit the divisions of the 15th Army guarding Calais, because new intelligence reports led him to believe, once again, that a second Allied landing was being planned. The success of the FORTITUDE deception plan went on and on: false information fed to the Germans by Allied agents resulted in colossal overestimates of the number of Allied divisions waiting in Britain. The Germans believed there were at least 57. In reality, at the time Cherbourg fell there were only 16 divisions plus a handful of British

FORTITUDE: A CONTINUING BOON

training divisions, which were intended as replacements for the 2nd Army. In late June the Germans still had more divisions guarding other sectors of the French coast than they had facing the Allied bridgehead. Even Rommel had come to accept that a second landing north of the Seine was now probable.

THE ODON OFFENSIVE

While the Germans were still preparing their attack Montgomery forestalled them by launching an offensive. His plan was to push south along a 15 km (9 mile) front in the British sector west of Caen in a bid to cross the River Odon and swing eastwards to outflank the city. The Odon is a tributary of the Orne, flowing towards Caen from the southwest, immediately south of the road that runs from the city to Villers-Bocage. The operation was code-named EPSOM, after the famous English Derby racecourse, and was assigned to the newly formed British VIII Corps under the command of Lieutenant General Sir Richard O'Connor. O'Connor's corps was composed of three divisions: the 43rd Wessex, the 15th Scottish and the 11th Armoured. Initially they would be supported

EPSOM

Right: A German 88-mm gun in action. Originally designed as an antiaircraft gun, the 88 was later adapted for use as a low trajectory tank killer. Its armour-piercing shells made it a most deadly battlefield weapon.

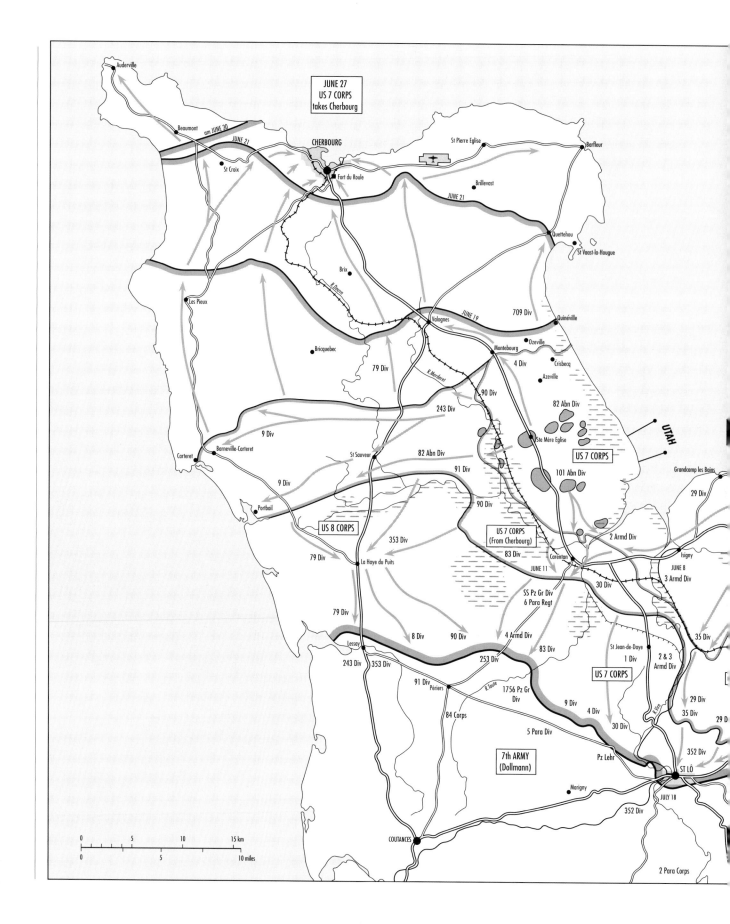

JUNE 27
US 7 CORPS
takes Cherbourg

Auderville

Beaumont

am JUNE 30

JUNE 21

CHERBOURG

St Croix

Fort du Roule

St Pierre Eglise

Barfleur

Brillevast

JUNE 21

Quettehou

St Vaast-la-Hougue

Brix

R. Divie

Les Pieux

JUNE 19

709 Div

Quinéville

Valognes

Bricquebec

Ozeville

Montebourg

4 Div

Crisbecq

79 Div

R. Merderet

Azeville

90 Div

82 Abn Div

243 Div

Ste Mère Eglise

UTAH

9 Div

US 7 CORPS

Carteret

Barneville-Carteret

St Sauveur

82 Abn Div

101 Abn Div

Grandcamp les Bains

91 Div

9 Div

90 Div

29 Div

Portbail

US 8 CORPS

353 Div

US 7 CORPS
(From Cherbourg)

2 Armd Div

79 Div

La Haye du Puits

83 Div

Carentan

Isigny

JUNE 11

JUNE 8

3 Armd Div

30 Div

SS Pz Gr Div
6 Para Regt

35 Div

79 Div

8 Div

90 Div

4 Armd Div

83 Div

St Jean-de-Daye

1 Div

2 & 3
Armd Div

Lessay

243 Div   353 Div

253 Div

US 7 CORPS

91 Div   Périers

R. Taute

9 Div

4 Div

29 Div

84 Corps

1756 Pz Gr
Div

30 Div

R. Vire

35 Div

29 D

5 Para Div

352 Div

7th ARMY
(Dollmann)

Pz Lehr

ST LÔ

Marigny

JULY 18

352 Div

0   5   10   15 km

0   5   10 miles

COUTANCES

2 Para Corps

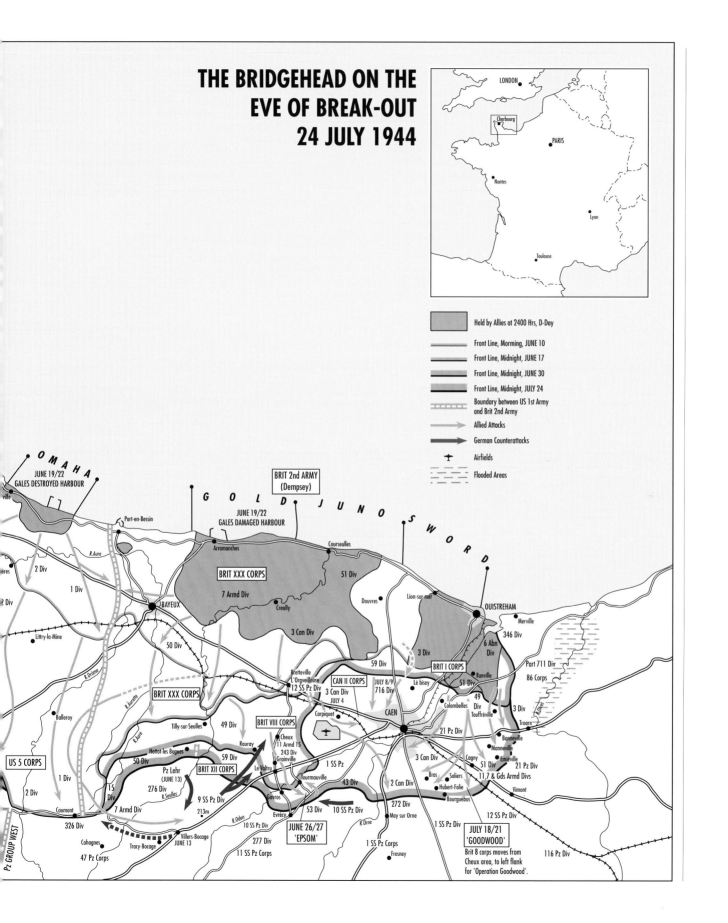

THE BRIDGEHEAD ON THE EVE OF BREAK-OUT 24 JULY 1944

LONDON

Cherbourg

PARIS

Nantes

Lyon

Toulouse

Held by Allies at 2400 Hrs, D-Day

Front Line, Morning, JUNE 10

Front Line, Midnight, JUNE 17

Front Line, Midnight, JUNE 30

Front Line, Midnight, JULY 24

Boundary between US 1st Army and Brit 2nd Army

Allied Attacks

German Counterattacks

Airfields

Flooded Areas

OMAHA
JUNE 19/22
GALES DESTROYED HARBOUR

ville

GOLD

BRIT 2nd ARMY
(Dempsey)

JUNO

SWORD

Port-en-Bessin

JUNE 19/22
GALES DAMAGED HARBOUR

Arromanches

Courseulles

R.Aure

2 Div

1 Div

2 Div

BRIT XXX CORPS

7 Armd Div

51 Div

Douvres

Lion-sur-mer

OUISTREHAM

Merville

BAYEUX

Creully

3 Can Div

346 Div

Littry-la-Mine

50 Div

59 Div

3 Div

6 Abn Div

Part 711 Div

86 Corps

R.Drôme

Bretteville
L'Orgveilleuse
12 SS Pz Div

CAN II CORPS
3 Can Div
JULY 4

JULY 8/9
716 Div

Lé bisey

BRIT I CORPS

Ranville

51 Div

R.Aurette

BRIT XXX CORPS

Carpiquet

CAEN

Colombelles

49 Div

Touffréville

3 Div

R.Orne

Balleroy

Tilly-sur-Seulles

49 Div

BRIT VIII CORPS

21 Pz Div

Banneville

Manneville

Troarn

US 5 CORPS

R.Aure

Hottot-les-Bogues

50 Div

59 Div

Rauray

Cheux
11 Armd 15
243 Div
Grainville

Le Valtru

1 SS Pz

3 Can Div

Cagny

51 Div

Emieville

21 Pz Div

1 Div

Pz Lehr
(JUNE 13)

BRIT XII CORPS

Tourmauville

43 Div

2 Can Div

Bras

Soliers

11,7 & Gds Armd Divs

Vimont

2 Div

15 Div

276 Div

R.Seulles

9 SS Pz Div

213m

Gavros

Evrécy

53 Div

10 SS Pz Div

May sur Orne

Hubert-Folie

Bourguébus

272 Div

12 SS Pz Div

Caumont

7 Armd Div

R.Odon

10 SS Pz Div

JUNE 26/27
'EPSOM'

R.Orne

1 SS Pz Div

JULY 18/21
'GOODWOOD'
Brit 8 corps moves from Cheux area, to left flank for 'Operation Goodwood'.

326 Div

Cahagnes

Tracy-Bocage

Villers-Bocage
JUNE 13

277 Div

11 SS Pz Corps

1 SS Pz Corps

Fresney

116 Pz Div

47 Pz Corps

Pz GROUP WEST

on their right by the 49th and 50th divisions of Bucknall's XXX Corps, which had been pushing south from Tilly-sur-Seulles.

25 JUNE

The British attack began on 25 June. The infantry moved forward in appalling weather conditions: dense mist followed by torrential rain. Soon the Normandy countryside was turned into a sea of mud that resembled the Flanders battlefields of World War I. Fighting all the way against determined resistance from the infantry of 12th SS Panzer, the British advanced through Cheux and Grain-ville towards the Odon. On 27 June the Germans, who had been caught off guard, launched an armoured counterattack which was quickly broken up by British antitank

BRITISH ADVANCE

guns. The 49th Division on the right captured Rauray after bitter fighting, while the 11th Armoured Division succeeded in seizing a bridge over the Odon. In no time British tanks were across the river and pressing south with all due speed.

The Germans were seriously alarmed and Rommel ordered all available reserves to be thrown in to halt the British thrust. The three Panzer divisions of General Hausser's Second Panzer Corps that had been earmarked for the drive to the coast were now concentrated upon the 2nd Army front. Dempsey became worried that this mass of armour might cut off the British armoured formations on the south side of the river. The forward tanks of the 11th Armoured were linked to the main bridgehead only by a narrow corridor, which at one point was less than 3 km (2 miles) wide and was held by the infantry of the 15th Scottish Division. Dempsey therefore made the decision, with Montgomery's approval, to withdraw his armour to a defensive position along the Odon and await the German counterattack.

THE BATTLE OF THE SCOTTISH CORRIDOR

So began the action that became known as the battle of the Scottish Corridor. On 29 June, on Hitler's orders, the German panzers attacked the narrow salient on both flanks –

but the British were ready. O'Connor had deployed his antitank guns and armour in prepared positions and when the panzers attacked they suffered heavy losses. The SS Grenadiers that went in behind the panzers were routed by the Scottish infantry and the German attack was called off. Two days later, on 1 July, Hausser's Panzer Corps made one last attempt to break through the corridor from the west. It was a powerful and determined assault by units of four panzer divisions, but the British line held and the German attack petered out, broken by concentrated British artillery fire.

1 JULY

D-Day – A Personal Memory

We climbed down the toggle ropes on the side of the ship and jumped into the assault craft. There were about 38 of us plus our piper, playing a battle tune. No-one spoke at all. We were tossed about like a cork in the sea and we all felt pretty sick and couldn't have cared less about the Jerries as we headed in towards the beach. Then we hit the sand. The water was over our shoulders as we dashed forward to take cover in the sand dunes. My first night I shared a trench with three dead Germans. Then we were machine gunned and dive bombed by two German planes which had earlier glided in with engines shut off and hit an ammunition ship which blew up, lighting up the whole area. Every anti-aircraft gun then opened up – an unbelievable sight from land and sea.

Mike Hannon, 8th Battalion, the King's Liverpool Regiment, attached to the 3rd Canadian Division

Right: British tanks moving through cornfields for the final attack on Caen.

In spite of their undoubted success against the panzers, O'Connor's divisions were ordered to break off the action and the British drive to outflank Caen from the west was never pressed home. For this reason Montgomery came in for considerable criticism from the Allied Supreme Command, especially from Eisenhower, who regarded the Odon offensive as a tactical failure in that little ground had been gained and that the capture of Caen seemed as remote as ever. The Germans, however, took a very different view. Montgomery's spoiling attack had inflicted upon them serious losses in both men and tanks, losses Rommel knew he could ill afford. Not only did EPSOM finish any chance of the planned German counteroffensive, but it used up most of Rommel's reserves and made it virtually impossible for the Germans to continue to hold Caen.

Eisenhower had no idea of the state of despair into which Montgomery's limited offensive had thrown the German High Command. Rommel even went so far as to suggest to Hitler that the German armies, including those in southern France, should withdraw to a new defensive line running from the Seine to Switzerland. If they did not

MONTGOMERY CRITICIZED

GERMAN DISMAY

withdraw, Rommel insisted, the 7th Army in Normandy would be destroyed and the 15th Army would be powerless to resist a second Allied landing. Hitler, however, flatly refused to allow a tactical withdrawal. He still believed that the Allied bridgehead could continue to be fenced in and he promised to commit more of the *Luftwaffe*'s dwindling reserve of aircraft to protect 7th Army supply routes. Von Rundstedt, now in almost open revolt, spoke bluntly about the need to make peace and was immediately dismissed from his post. On 2 July Field Marshal von Kluge, one of Hitler's most servile and compliant generals, took over command in the west.

HITLER REFUSES WITHDRAWAL

VON RUNDSTEDT DISMISSED

IMPASSE

By the first week of July 1944 the situation in Normandy appeared to be one of stalemate. Bradley's 1st Army, in spite of its growing numerical superiority, was making little progress in its push southwards out of the Cotentin, meeting bitter resistance around La Haye-du-Puits and the Forest of Mont Castre. The Americans were also finding it impossible to break the stubborn German hold on St Lô. Similarly, the British and Canadians could not break through the entrenched German positions around Caen. A break-out from the bridgehead seemed as far away as ever. But although there was little for the Allies to cheer about, the truth was that the German forces in Normandy were being steadily worn down.

A major reason for this was the overwhelming Allied air superiority. In 1940 it had been the Germans who enjoyed command of the skies, their Stuka dive bombers spreading chaos and terror among the retreating French and British armies. Now it was the turn of the *Wehrmacht* to suffer the misery and frustration of non-stop air attack, as swarms of Allied Mustangs, Typhoons and Spitfires ranged unchallenged and with no

ALLIED AIR SUPERIORITY

let-up over the battlefield, shooting everything that moved on the ground. The German infantry, tough and disciplined though it was, began at last to show signs of cracking under the continuous strain.

Another potent weapon for the Allies was their big naval guns, which from the start of the invasion played an important part in supporting the ground forces in the bridgehead. The Germans were awed by the massive carpet of fire which could be laid by the British and American battleships and cruisers stationed offshore. Even the elite panzer troops, accustomed to heavy artillery barrages on the Russian front, found the hard

EFFECT OF ALLIED NAVAL GUNS

pounding by the large calibre naval guns an unexpectedly terrifying experience. Panzer columns were often pinned down for hours by the merciless shelling. In fact, one of Rommel's reasons for wanting to withdraw his troops further inland was to put them out of range of the Allied warships. The role of the Allied navies in helping to break down the German resistance cannot be overestimated.

THE AIR BOMBARDMENT

With the Allied armies bogged down right along the front, Montgomery decided after all to take Caen by frontal assault, and for

Below: Canadian infantry fighting amid the ruins of Caen as they try to clear the Germans from the ravaged city.

this he called in the heavy bombers of Air Chief Marshal Harris's RAF Bomber Command. On the night of 7 July close on 500 RAF Halifaxes and Lancasters carpeted the northern outskirts of Caen with high explosive bombs. The destruction was terrible. The city was effectively reduced to ruins. But this sledgehammer blow was in many ways futile, causing more casualties among French civilians than it did among the Germans, most of whom were entrenched in the villages north of the bombing limit. The following day British I Corps attacked, aiming to penetrate through the city and seize the river crossings over the Orne. The two British divisions, the 59th and the 3rd, came in from the north, fighting every step of the way in the teeth of fierce resistance by SS Panzer Grenadiers. Meanwhile the Canadian 3rd Division attacked Caen from the west. By 9 July most of what was left of the ancient Norman city was in British hands, but the Germans continued to hold the southern suburbs on the far bank of the Orne and had blown all the river bridges. Caen had fallen but the British had gained little by its capture. Montgomery's intended advance to the south and east had been thwarted and he could not secure access to the main roads which fan out towards Falaise and Paris. Room to manoeuvre his cramped forces had been denied him. The Allies remained pinned within their narrow bridgehead, which at no point covered a distance of more than 32 km (20 miles) from the sea.

Painful and bloody though it was, the drive on Caen had the strategic purpose of diverting the Germans' attention away from the American front, allowing Bradley's forces time to build up for an eventual break-out. Bradley later wrote, 'We desperately wanted the Germans to believe this attack on Caen was the main Allied effort'. There is no doubt that the Germans did. On 11 July, of the eight panzer divisions in Normandy, seven and a

7 JULY

CAEN IN RUINS

MONTGOMERY
FRUSTRATED

11 JULY

half were lined up against the British front. Moreover, during the previous week, four fresh German infantry divisions had been moved to Normandy, three of them to face the British and Canadians. Montgomery's basic strategy of holding the enemy in the east and preparing a hammer blow by the Americans in the west was working. But the cost in British lives was heavy. The ratio of casualties among the infantry was approximately three to one in the Germans' favour, a rate of loss Montgomery knew could not be allowed to continue. British manpower reserves were, by this stage of the war, almost exhausted. Unlike the Americans, who had fresh divisions waiting to cross the Atlantic, the British were running short of men to replace their front line casualties. Montgomery knew that there would be no more divisions for his 2nd Army, and that sobering thought undoubtedly influenced his military thinking from this point onwards.

GOODWOOD

In the second week of July the persistent pressure of the US forces in the west of the bridgehead began to tell. The Americans now had the best part of 14 divisions along their 80 km (50 mile) front. The Germans facing them had for a time only six, although reinforcements were soon on the way. On 8 July the important road junction of La Haye-du-Puits in the western Cotentin fell at last to the US 7th Corps. Ten days later, after savage fighting, units of the 35th and 29th divisions of the US 19th Corps battled their way into St Lô in the deep valley of the River Vire. German attention at once switched to the American front, where a serious threat was developing, and two panzer divisions, the 2nd SS and the remnants of the badly mauled Panzer Lehr, moved west to oppose Bradley.

Still anxious to divert the Germans' attention from the Cotentin, where Bradley was

preparing his major attack, Montgomery informed Eisenhower of his intention to launch a new offensive on the eastern flank. Code-named GOODWOOD (like EPSOM, the name of an English racecourse), the plan was to make a powerful armoured thrust from the small bridgehead east of the Orne held by the British 6th Airborne. The aim was to bypass Caen on the east, seize the high ground around Bourguébus ridge, fan out to the south and east and improve the Allied position beyond the Orne. The Germans, however, had anticipated the threat. Unknown to the British, they had prepared a very strong defence zone 16 km (10 miles) deep with infantry, antitank guns and panzer support.

GOODWOOD began on 18 July, the same day that St Lô fell to the Americans. Three armoured divisions, the 11th and 7th Armoured and the Guards, attacked southwards from the Orne crossing at Bénouville towards Cagny. At the same time the 3rd

Above: British and Canadian troops move through the rubble-strewn streets of Caen after its capture on 9 July 1944. The historic cathedral was severely damaged during the battle.

LA HAYE-DU-PUITS

ST LÔ FALLS

18 JULY

A MASSIVE
BOMBARDMENT

Canadian and 3rd British Infantry Divisions attacked along the flanks of the armour. The offensive was preceded by a massive aerial and artillery bombardment, which left the German defenders temporarily dazed. But they quickly recovered and fought back furiously. Although suffering heavy losses, they succeeded in knocking out about 400 British tanks, most of which were quickly replaced. Three days later, after fierce fighting amid drenching rain, the British attack was halted. The enemy had been pushed back between 6 and 11 km (4 and 7 miles) to the south and east of Caen and the Canadians had cleared the Germans from the southern Caen suburbs. Montgomery declared himself more than satisfied. The Allied Supreme Command, however, had been wrongly expecting a British break-out into the the Falaise plain to the south-east. For this reason GOODWOOD was deemed a failure and Montgomery came in for more heavy criticism both from the British and Americans. The deputy Supreme Commander, Air Chief-Marshal Tedder, who had little grasp of the true nature of the fighting, was furious at Montgomery's lack of progress in the campaign.

Meanwhile, Field Marshal Rommel was out of the battle. He had been severely injured when his car crashed after being attacked by British fighters and was later sent back to Germany to recover. In his final report to Hitler, Rommel stated bluntly that an Allied breakthrough was only a matter of time. 'The unequal struggle', he wrote, 'is nearing its end.' The Desert Fox's prediction was to be proved right.

**STORM OVER
GOODWOOD**

ROMMEL INJURED

Right: A British soldier gives a helping hand to an old lady in the devastated centre of Caen after the battle. The few French civilians who remained in the city described how the retreating Germans deliberately destroyed buildings that had not been damaged in the fighting.

CHAPTER TWENTY

Break-out

COBRA

At last, in the fourth week of July 1944, the Normandy struggle reached its turning point. On 25 July – 49 days after the D-Day landings – General Bradley launched his long awaited offensive. Its deadly intent was appropriately summed up in its code-name: COBRA.

The American build-up in the Cotentin peninsula had reached bursting point. There was scarcely room in the bridgehead to accommodate the masses of troops, tanks and artillery that were piling up. In addition to the 15 divisions of the 1st Army, there were four divisions of General Patton's arriving US 3rd Army waiting in reserve. Facing the Americans were elements of about 9 divisions which included more than a hundred tanks. The German forces at this point had been split into two armies: the 7th Army, commanded by General Hausser, on the American front, and the 14 divisions of the newly designated 5th Panzer Army, commanded by General Hans Eberbach, facing the British.

Bradley planned to concentrate his attack on a narrow 6-km (4-mile) front along the St Lô-Périers road just northwest of St Lô. Three American infantry divisions of General Lawton Collins' 7th Corps were to make the initial assault, followed by two armoured divisions and one of motorized infantry.

However, COBRA began disastrously. The American offensive, like the British Operation GOODWOOD, was preceded by a devastating bombing attack designed to annihilate the German front line defences. Waves of bombers and fighter bombers of the American 8th and 9th Air Forces laid a carpet of high explosive over an area of roughly 20 sq km (8 sq miles). Unfortunately, the Liberators, Flying Fortresses and Thunderbolts bombed grievously short, causing severe casualties among the infantry assault divisions. More than one hundred men were killed, including a lieutenant general. When he learned of the catastrophe, Bradley was beside himself with helpless rage.

But, if the air attack was terrifying for the American ground troops, for the Germans it was like a vision of hell. Panzer Lehr's commander, General Bayerlein, described the German front line as resembling a moonscape. 'Seventy per cent of my personnel were out of action – dead, wounded, crazed or numbed. All my front line tanks were knocked out.'

For two days COBRA made only slight progress against what appeared to be solid German opposition. The Americans advanced about 6 km (4 miles) from the start line, taking the villages of Marigny and St Gilles. Then, on 27 July, Bradley began to realize that the German defence was crumbling. The 2nd Armored Division pushed south to Canisy and occupied the high ground at Le Mesnil Herman, 11 km (7 miles) south of St Lô. The moment to exploit the breach had come. Supported by dive bombers of the 9th Tactical Air Force, the 1st (Motorized) Infantry and 3rd Armored divisions swung west to threaten the town of Coutances. At the same

Left: The American offensive COBRA in full swing. US motorized infantry enter Marigny during the drive on the important town of Coutances on the western side of the Cotentin peninsula.

A diary extract, 7 June 1944

Woke up at 0600 hours and found we had arrived off the coast during the night. The Chief Engineer was feeling sad as this ship had to die. For after we had been off-loaded she was due to be sunk to form a harbour together with other old cargo ships. The sea was very rough and I felt rough too. The air was rent with the thunder of the heavy guns of the warships firing shorewards. The salvoes of the rocket ships were impressive. At 2pm I went down the rope ladder onto the landing craft that was to take us ashore. The sea all around was being peppered with shell bursts, and I was really nervous as I could not swim. We had a dry-shod landing, driving ashore in the CO's car. On French soil again for the first time since June 1 1940. Shells bursting on the beach, a very excited Camp Commandant giving orders, dead bodies everywhere and prisoners being herded in batches. We drove to the assembly area to find out what was to be done next. The village was Ouistreham, the sector SWORD, the beach section Queen. The French civilians we met were delighted to see us and pinned roses on our battle-dress, offering us glasses of wine. I don't know how these people managed to survive all the shelling. We drove inland and headed for Caen but were stopped by a Military Policeman at a crossroads and directed to Colleville, where Divisional HQ had been set up. At 8.30pm we unloaded the car and set up our office in a wooden hut filled with wheelbarrows. There was a lot of sniping and I was feeling nervy. Managed to get a German steel helmet as a trophy before having something to eat from my pack and then sleeping out under a tree. Continuous firing from tanks and field guns. It was the noisiest night of my life.

Ernest Bayley, Corporal in the 3rd British Infantry Divisional Signals

Right: Troops and self-propelled guns of the US 3rd Army push into Brittany following the break-out from Avranches. A knocked out German tank lies in the ditch by the roadside.

time General Troy Middleton's 8th Corps, which had been held up by the German 84th Corps around Lessay and Périers, suddenly broke through from the north. Coutances was captured and four American armoured divisions were on the move. In order to speed up their progress through the *bocage*, American engineers had fitted steel blades, known as Rhinos, to the front of their Sherman tanks, which enabled them to slice into the banks below the thick hedgerows and rip open a path through which the tank could drive. The Rhinos proved a godsend, allowing the American armour a freedom of

COUTANCES

RHINOS

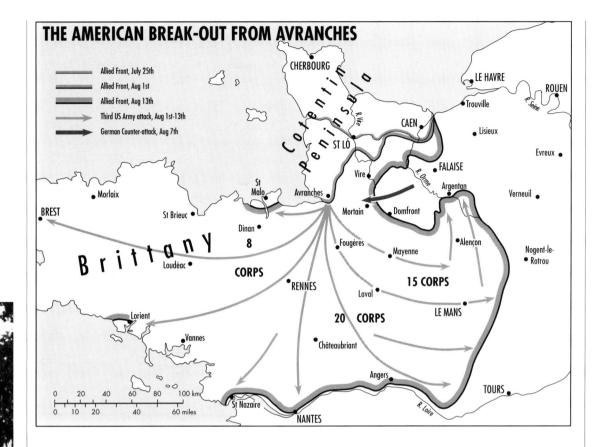

THE AMERICAN BREAK-OUT FROM AVRANCHES

Allied Front, July 25th
Allied Front, Aug 1st
Allied Front, Aug 13th
Third US Army attack, Aug 1st–13th
German Counter-attack, Aug 7th

CHERBOURG · LE HAVRE · ROUEN · Trouville · R. Seine · Cotentin peninsula · R. Vire · CAEN · Lisieux · ST LÔ · Evreux · Vire · FALAISE · R. Orme · Argentan · St Malo · Avranches · Mortain · Domfront · Alençon · Verneuil · Morlaix · BREST · St Brieuc · Dinan · Fougères · Mayenne · Nogent-le-Rotrou · Brittany · 8 CORPS · Loudéac · RENNES · Laval · 15 CORPS · LE MANS · Lorient · 20 CORPS · Vannes · Châteaubriant · Angers · TOURS · St Nazaire · NANTES · R. Loire

0 20 40 60 80 100 km
0 10 20   40   60 miles

manoeuvre that they exploited to the full. By the morning of 29 July the German front in the Cotentin was disintegrating and American columns were sweeping south. Bradley was on the verge of a major victory and the Allied break-out was at last in sight.

PATTON

It was at this moment, with the German western flank collapsing, that Bradley decided to unleash General Patton. Patton's 3rd Army was not due to become operational until 1 August, but Bradley, keenly aware of Patton's flair for rapid movement and exploitation, gave him immediate control of US 8th Corps. Patton needed no urging. Mobile warfare was what he understood and he seized his chance with both hands. He ordered the 4th and 6th Armored Divisions of 8th Corps to go flat out. On 30 July the spearheads of the 4th Armored had reached

Avranches, in the southwest corner of the Cotentin peninsula. The following day a combat group of the division seized the vital bridge over the River Sélune at Pontaubault, just south of Avranches. Patton's tanks had broken out of the confines of the peninsula, of the *bocage* and of Normandy. The Americans were poised to turn the corner and strike westwards into Brittany. The whole of northwest France lay open to them.

On 1 and 2 August the American break-out was in full swing. The 4th Armored Division was racing across the Brittany peninsula to capture Rennes while other armoured formations and motorized infantry headed west towards the Atlantic port of Brest and south towards Nantes at the mouth of the Loire. Patton now started to move the fresh divisions of his waiting 3rd Army through the tight bottleneck at Avranches and out into Brittany. There was hardly anything to stop them. Much of the peninsula was already in

BREAK-OUT

1 AND 2 AUGUST

Left: The advance towards Flers. A British light Bren gun-carrier passes through the town of Tinchebray on the boundary between the British and US Armies. Troops are seen talking to French civilians in the background. Note the sign: 'British troops turn left'; Allied units were carefully marshalled by military police to avoid confusion.

BREST

the hands of the French Resistance, and the remaining German forces there retreated rapidly towards the port of Brest, which, on Hitler's orders, was turned into a fortress. Brest held out for another seven weeks, its garrison eventually surrendering to the Americans on 18 September.

With Patton's 3rd Army sweeping south and west through the Avranches corridor, the US 1st Army attacked to the east to protect the line of the break-out. The important town

MORTAIN

of Mortain, some 27 km (17 miles) east of Avranches, was captured by the US 7th Corps on 2 August and the American front started to pivot round from the point just west of Caumont, where it linked up with the British.

In the meantime Montgomery had switched his armour from the Caen sector to near Caumont and ordered British VIII and

BRITISH THRUST

XXX Corps to push south in support of the American offensive. VIII Corps, including the Guards and the 11th Armoured Divisions and

the 3rd and 15th Infantry divisions, successfully took Le Bény Bocage and swung southeast along a line threatening the towns of Condé and Flers. The British thrust was finally checked, but not before it had drawn into battle the 2nd SS Panzer Corps, which was being diverted to intervene on the American front. Von Kluge was in despair. The Allied front in Normandy was now wheeling, as Montgomery and Bradley had originally planned, into a line facing directly towards the Seine and Paris. Von Kluge had no means of checking the American break-out and his position was critical.

LE BENY BOCAGE

FOUR ARMIES

At the beginning of August the Allied command structure underwent some important changes. With the emergence of the US 3rd Army under the control of General Patton, General Bradley was moved up to become

BRADLEY

the overall commander of both 1st and 3rd Armies, which were to become known as 12th Army Group. It was an awkward situation for Bradley who, a year earlier, in Sicily, had been Patton's subordinate. Now the roles were reversed. Bradley did not like Patton, whose vanity and bravado he found deeply distasteful, but he was a shrewd soldier who put the task of winning before differences of personality. He valued Patton's unique qualities and he used them to advantage. Lieutenant General Courtney Hodges took over from Bradley as commander of the 1st Army. While on the British front the Canadians were

formed into a separate army – 1st Canadian – under the command of Lieutenant General H.D.G. Crerar. It was composed of the Canadian 2nd Corps and the three divisions of British I Corps, to which the 1st Polish Armoured Division was added. From then on the British 2nd and Canadian 1st Armies became 21st Army Group.

MORTAIN

The Normandy battle was effectively decided by two moves made in the first week of August, one on the Allied side, one on the

Left: General George S. Patton, commander of the US 3rd Army, leaving his tent to talk to war correspondents. Patton's drive and unstoppable self-confidence were instrumental in exploiting the success of the American break-out.

German. The original Allied plan had called for Patton's American 3rd Army to liberate Brittany and secure the ports. But the ease with which the 3rd Army columns were driving virtually unopposed to the Atlantic coast made both Patton and Bradley think again. It seemed to them pointless wasting a whole army in Brittany when the main enemy strength was in the east. On 3 August, therefore, Bradley took a decision that, as events proved, would alter the entire course of the battle. He ordered Patton to leave a minimum force in Brittany and switch his main strength to drive eastwards and turn the German left flank which was now totally exposed. It was a master stroke. Montgomery, when informed of the decision, at once endorsed it, recognizing that the success of the American break-out had changed the overall situation. Accordingly, Patton sent his divisions racing eastward in a wide sweep far to the south of the main German armies concentrated in Normandy. Without worrying about mopping up pockets of resistance, Patton's 15th Corps moved with lightning speed through the open French countryside past Laval and Mayenne towards Le Mans. Other columns of US 20th Corps fanned out southwards to seize the town of Angers on the River Loire, and were soon moving east towards Tours.

3 AUGUST

A MASTER STROKE

Faced with this dangerous encircling move by Patton's divisions, the only sensible German response would have been to withdraw eastwards to a new defence line along the Seine, but Hitler refused to allow any retreat. Instead, on 4 August, he ordered von Kluge to assemble all the panzers he could muster and launch an attack towards Mortain. The aim was to drive a wedge through to the sea at Avranches and so cut off the 3rd Army. It might on the face of it have seemed a brilliant counterstroke, but von Kluge realized that such a move spelled the destruction of the German armies in Normandy. Although

aghast at Hitler's plan, von Kluge dared not refuse to obey his leader's command.

The German counterattack began on the night of 6 August. General Hans von Funck's 47th Panzer Corps, comprising around 185 tanks and assault guns, broke through the American lines just north of Mortain, eventually recapturing the town and advancing 11 km (7 miles) towards Avranches. Although a powerful attack, it did not have the strength that Hitler had intended as British pressure between Caen and Vire prevented the Germans from moving more than one panzer division to the American front. Bradley, moveover, sensing the possibility of a German counterthrust around Mortain, had carefully positioned divisions of the 1st Army on the hills just north and northwest of the town. The 30th Division of the US 7th Corps bore the brunt of the German attack, one of its battalions fighting a courageous action to hold the key heights of Hill 317, which was surrounded for five days. Collins later described the defence of this hilltop by the 120th Infantry Regiment as one of the outstanding small unit actions of the entire war.

The stubborn, brave defence put up by the GIs of the 30th Division was instrumental in

6 AUGUST: COUNTERATTACK

HILL 317

Left: American tanks
with infantry in
support engaged in
heavy fighting near
St Lô at the start of
the COBRA offensive.

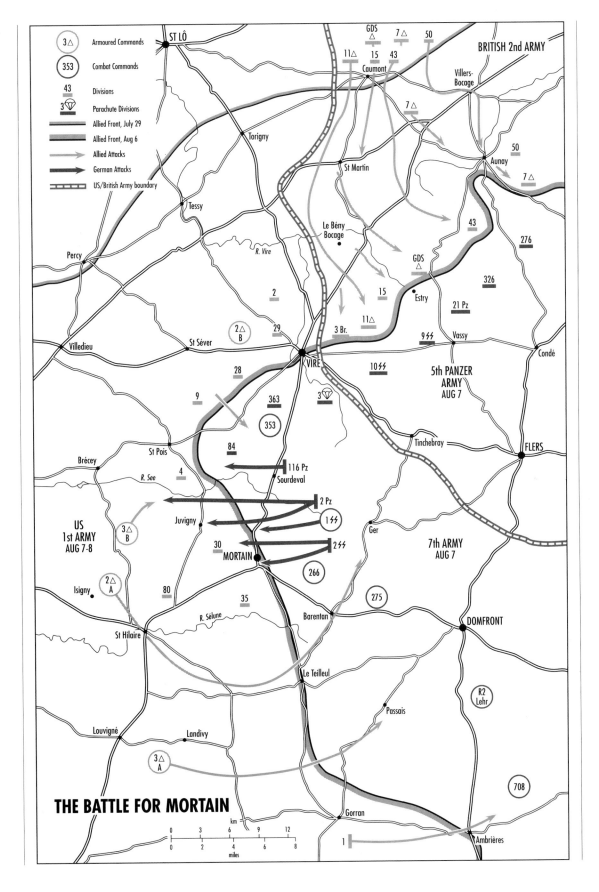

THE BATTLE FOR MORTAIN

Armoured Commands 3△

Combat Commands 353

Divisions 43

Parachute Divisions 3

Allied Front, July 29

Allied Front, Aug 6

Allied Attacks

German Attacks

US/British Army boundary

ST LÔ

GDS

7△

50

BRITISH 2nd ARMY

11△

15

43

Caumont

Villers-
Bocage

Torigny

7△

Aunay

50

St Martin

7△

Tessy

Le Bény
Bocage

R. Vire

43

276

Percy

GDS

326

2

15

Estry

21 Pz

St Séver

2△
B

29

3 Br.

11△

9

Vassy

Condé

Villedieu

VIRE

10

5th PANZER
ARMY
AUG 7

28

9

363

3

Tinchebray

FLERS

St Pois

353

84

Brécey

R. See

4

116 Pz
Sourdeval

2 Pz

US
1st ARMY
AUG 7-8

3△
B

Juvigny

1

Ger

7th ARMY
AUG 7

30

MORTAIN

2

266

Isigny

2△
A

80

35

275

DOMFRONT

R. Sélune

Barentan

St Hilaire

Le Teilleul

R2
Lehr

Passais

Louvigné

Landivy

3△
A

708

Gorran

Ambrières

km
0   3   6   9   12

0   2   4   6   8
miles

43rd Wessex Division. On 7 August the British 59th (Staffordshire) Division succeeded in forcing a crossing of the Orne close to Thury Harcourt and was poised to push eastwards out of the dense *bocage* towards the open Falaise plain.

That same night the Canadian 2nd Corps, commanded by Lieutenant General Guy

PANZERS: SITTING TARGETS

blunting the German offensive. Meanwhile, the panzers, strung out along the roads around Mortain, were becoming an easy target for American Thunderbolts and rocket-firing RAF Typhoons, which hammered the German armoured columns. Still Hitler refused to call off the attack; on the contrary, he decided to reinforce it. He not only ordered a further two panzer divisions to be moved west from the British front, but he also ordered the 9th Panzer to move from Le Mans to Mortain to join the offensive. Since the 9th Panzer was one of only two divisions standing between Patton's spearheads and the Seine, the desperation on the German side was apparent. General Hausser protested to von Kluge over the recklessness in moving this division, but to no avail; Hitler was prepared to stake everything in his frantic bid to capture Avranches.

THE TRAP

With the German forces being sucked into the savage fighting around Mortain, the Allies began to tighten the pressure on their flanks. British XXX Corps, pushing southeast from Aunay, seized the important heights of Mont Pinçon, some 330 m (1,100 ft) high, after a heroic and bloody assault by infantry of the

MONT PINÇON

Left: German SS Panzer Grenadiers on the alert for any sign of enemy movement. These tough troops formed the infantry support units of the panzer divisions.

Simonds, launched a renewed attack southwards from Caen towards Falaise. The Corps, comprising the 2nd Canadian Division and the British 51st Highland Scottish Division, moved in six long columns of tanks, motorized infantry and artillery behind a rolling artillery barrage. Behind them came the tanks of two armoured divisions, the 4th Canadian and the 1st Polish, which were going into action for the first time. This operation, code-named TOTALISE, was to form the northern jaw of the trap that was designed to close around the 7th Army. Its southern jaw was to be Patton's 3rd Army, which was to swing north in a right hook through Alençon and on to the town of Argentan,

TOTALISE

Left: War in the *bocage*. American troops concealed on the edge of a wooded hilltop overlooking German positions. The picture vividly illustrates the type of country which characterized the Normandy fighting.

Left: Some of the thousands of German prisoners taken by the Allies during the bloody battle of the Falaise pocket. The battle resulted in the virtual destruction of the German 7th Army and the 5th Panzer Army.

26 km (16 miles) southeast of Falaise. While, much to Montgomery's dismay, the Canadian advance turned out to be disappointingly slow, Patton's thrust was rapid. On 12 August the US 15th Corps captured Alençon and was closing around Argentan well to the rear of the German 7th Army. Barely 32 km (20 miles) now separated the Americans from the Canadians. If they could join up, the Germans would be encircled.

THE FALAISE GAP

Too late the Germans realized the danger. Their forces in Normandy now occupied what amounted to a long salient roughly 65 km (40 miles) deep by 50 km (30 miles) wide with its arrowhead pointing towards Mortain. At last, on 16 August, von Kluge was allowed to issue the order to pull back. The 7th Army and the 5th Panzer Army at once began a fighting withdrawal, which rapidly

turned into a rout. The same day the Canadians finally battled their way into Falaise, cutting the gap between them and the Americans to a mere 24 km (15 miles).

The next three days saw the most terrible destruction of the German armies. As they struggled desperately to fight their way out of what was to become known as the Falaise pocket, they were subjected to constant shelling and aerial bombing which they were powerless to resist. Their columns of trucks, tanks, guns, cars and horse-drawn wagons became packed nose to tail in the narrow Normandy lanes, a sitting target for the Allied fighter bombers. A wholesale slaughter ensued as men and horses were blown to pieces in what was little more than a nightmarish killing ground.

Slowly, remorselessly, the trap closed around the Germans. On 19 August units of the 1st Polish Armoured Division and the US 90th Division met at Chambois on the River

ALENÇON

16 AUGUST:
GERMAN RETREAT

FALAISE

19 AUGUST

Dives 13 km (8 miles) northeast of Argentan. The gap was sealed, but the Germans did not give up. On 20 August General Hausser ordered the remnants of his panzer divisions inside the pocket to break out and for a few hours they succeeded. A hole was punched in the thin Canadian screen just north of Chambois and some German columns broke through to the east. Thousands of Germans managed to slip across the Dives and escape to safety – among them Hausser himself – before the Allies again closed the gap, this time for good.

By the last week of August, the Allied forces in Normandy numbered 38 divisions; 22 American, 11 British, three Canadian, one French and one Polish.

Below: The capture of Falaise. Canadian engineers search for mines as they enter the town on 18 August 1944.

AFTERMATH

The trail of destruction of the two German armies ran all the way from Mortain to the

villages of Trun and Chambois, where the last German escape route lay. The wreckage of tanks and guns, half-tracks and personnel carriers was scattered throughout the lanes and hedgerows of the *bocage*. The German dead lay in piles, along with the bloated hulks of dead horses, rotting in the summer heat. Over everything lay the stench of death. General Eisenhower, who entered the pocket a couple of days after the fighting ended, was sickened by the carnage, describing the scene as something from Dante's *Inferno*. It was, he said, 'possible to walk for hundreds of yards on nothing but dead and decaying flesh'.

Above: The ruined town of Falaise after its capture by the Canadians. Rubble from the shell-blasted houses litters the streets.

CHAPTER TWENTY-ONE

The Road to Victory

THE ALLIED TRIUMPH

GERMAN CASUALTIES

The battle of the Falaise pocket marked the end of the two-and-a-half-month-long Normandy campaign. More than 10,000 Germans were killed inside the pocket and about 50,000 taken prisoner, while losses in armoured vehicles, guns and other equipment were enormous. By 21 August the battered remnants of the eight surviving panzer divisions could muster no more than 77 tanks between them. During the whole of the Normandy fighting since D-Day 250,000 German troops had been killed or wounded, with another 200,000 taken prisoner. Altogether the best part of 40 German divisions had been destroyed.

ALLIED CASUALTIES

Allied losses in the Normandy fighting totalled approximately 209,000 ground troops killed, wounded or missing, of which 126,000 were American. The British and Canadians lost just under 16,000 killed; the Americans almost 21,000. In addition more than 8,000 RAF aircrew lost their lives and a similar number of American airmen.

A MAGNIFICENT VICTORY

It was a high price to pay but the Allies had won a magnificent victory. Against all the odds they had broken into Hitler's fortress Europe and liberated most of northern France. They had inflicted upon the German army the most crushing defeat it had experienced since Stalingrad, and what remained of the Nazi forces in France were in headlong retreat eastwards across the Seine. But in spite of this achievement some circles of the Allied High Command were dissatisfied. There was

DISSATISFACTION

anger that 20,000 German troops had managed to escape from the Falaise pocket, and both Montgomery and Bradley were criticized for alleged slowness in closing the gap. Military historians over the decades have debated this question and Montgomery in particular has come under scrutiny on both sides of the Atlantic over his handling of the campaign. With hindsight it is apparent that not everything went exactly according to plan. The Germans conducted a masterly and resolute defence. Their troops almost everywhere fought superbly, making the British and Americans struggle for every small advance. But Montgomery's policy of keeping the Germans 'off-balance' , as he liked to put it, undoubtedly paid dividends. His tactics for the most part were sound and his strategy of holding on the British front and breaking out on the American was ultimately proved correct, although its success owed much to the skill, decisiveness and quickness of perception shown by Bradley. Finally, of course, it can be argued – as many Germans later did – that the defeat was the greater because of the blind obstinacy of Adolf Hitler. His blunder in attempting to hold ground at all costs, and, in particular, his fatal decision to persist with the counterattack at Mortain, made the destruction of the German armies inevitable.

MONTGOMERY

HITLER

Those who fought in Normandy remember it as a grim and unrelenting struggle. For the ordinary Allied soldier – whether American, British or Canadian – the *bocage* was one long nightmare, where men were in constant

Right: The Allied pursuit begins. British armour in an endless column moves through the Normandy town of Lisieux heading east towards Rouen and the Seine. The magnificent cathedral in the background stands unharmed. American spearhead forces were already across the Seine south of Paris, a feat accomplished by Patton's 3rd Army on 19 August 1944.

Right: The liberation of Brussels, 3 September 1944. The scenes of jubilation as Belgians flock into the streets to greet the British columns as they enter the city. These happy girls have effectively taken over a British jeep in celebration.

fear from hidden snipers, mortar and artillery fire and wickedly concealed mines and booby traps. Death lurked in every wood, every hedgerow. To cross a lane or a gap in a hedge could spell disaster. Many Allied troops never actually saw a German unless it was a shattered corpse. They also did not realize that they had won until it was all over and the Germans in front of them had melted away. For the infantry, who bore the brunt of the fighting against a largely invisible enemy, the over-riding memory would be of extremes of drenching rain and mud on the one hand and blistering heat and flies on the other. The horrifying experience of seeing so many comrades cut down, often whole battalions decimated, would be etched in their consciousness for ever.

THE PURSUIT

After Falaise the pursuit of the fleeing Germans began in earnest. Patton's 3rd Army spearheads had already crossed the Seine on 19 August and by the 25th all four Allied

armies reached the river. Paris was liberated the same day, having been largely taken over by the French Resistance. To the delight of the Parisians American armoured columns headed by General Leclerc's 2nd French Armoured Division were sent by Bradley to take control of the city, and soon Free French tanks were rolling in triumph down the Champs Elysées.

The British and Canadians, so long bottled up in their narrow bridgehead around Caen, showed that they could directly rival Patton's speed of movement. While the Americans were driving east from Paris towards Metz and the German frontier, the British raced north-east towards Belgium. On 3 September, after a dash of 120 km (75 miles) in a single day, the Guards Armoured Division entered Brussels to a rapturous welcome from the citizens of Belgium's capital. No British soldier who took part in that liberation would ever forget the emotional scenes. Forced out of Belgium by the invading Nazis in 1940, the Tommies had come back. The Belgians went wild with joy and gratitude and the celebrations lasted

**25 AUGUST:
PARIS LIBERATED**

**3 SEPTEMBER:
BRUSSELS LIBERATED**

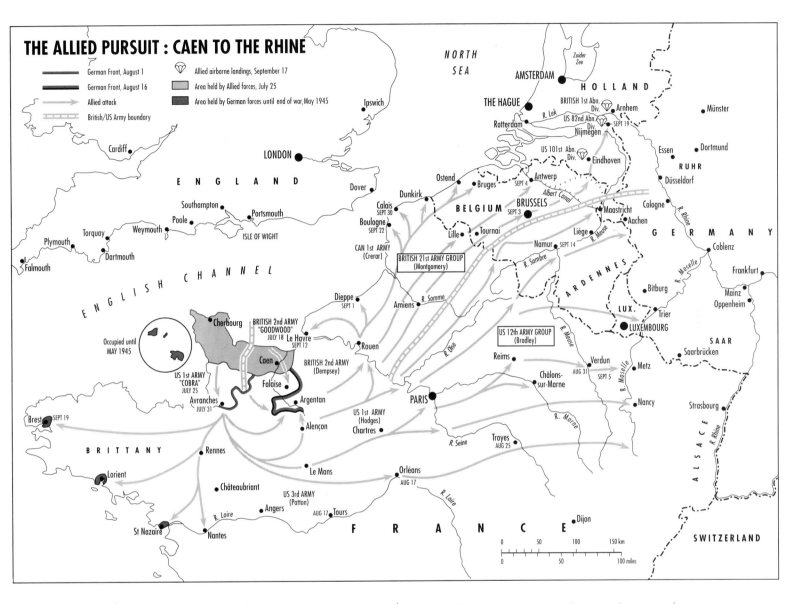

THE ALLIED PURSUIT : CAEN TO THE RHINE

German Front, August 1

German Front, August 16

Allied attack

British/US Army boundary

Allied airborne landings, September 17

Area held by Allied forces, July 25

Area held by German forces until end of war, May 1945

NORTH SEA

Zuider Zee

AMSTERDAM

HOLLAND

THE HAGUE

BRITISH 1st Abn. Div.

R. Lek

Arnhem

Münster

Rotterdam

US 82nd Abn Div.
SEPT 19

Nijmegen

Essen

Dortmund

Ipswich

US 101st Abn. Div.

Eindhoven

RUHR

Ostend

Antwerp

Düsseldorf

Cardiff

LONDON

E N G L A N D

Dover

Dunkirk

Bruges

SEPT 4

BELGIUM

BRUSSELS
SEPT 3

Albert Canal

Maastricht

Cologne

R. Rhine

Southampton

Portsmouth

Calais
SEPT 30

Boulogne
SEPT 22

Lille

Tournai

Liège

Aachen

G E R M A N Y

Poole

ISLE OF WIGHT

CAN 1st ARMY
(Crerar)

BRITISH 21st ARMY GROUP
(Montgomery)

Namur
SEPT 14

R. Meuse

Coblenz

Torquay

Weymouth

Plymouth

Dartmouth

Falmouth

E N G L I S H   C H A N N E L

Dieppe
SEPT 1

Amiens

R. Somme

R. Sambre

A R D E N N E S

R. Moselle

Bitburg

Frankfurt

Mainz

Oppenheim

LUX.

Trier

SAAR

Occupied until
MAY 1945

Cherbourg

BRITISH 2nd ARMY
"GOODWOOD"
JULY 18

Le Havre
SEPT 12

Rouen

R. Oise

US 12th ARMY GROUP
(Bradley)

R. Meuse

LUXEMBOURG

Saarbrücken

Caen

BRITISH 2nd ARMY
(Dempsey)

Reims

Verdun
AUG 31

R. Moselle

Metz

US 1st ARMY
"COBRA"
JULY 25

Falaise

Argentan

Châlons-
sur-Marne

SEPT 5

Nancy

Strasbourg

Avranches
JULY 31

Alençon

US 1st ARMY
(Hodges)

PARIS

R. Seine

R. Marne

A L S A C E

R. Rhine

Brest
SEPT 19

Chartres

Troyes
AUG 25

B R I T T A N Y

Rennes

Le Mans

Orléans
AUG 17

R. Loire

Lorient

Châteaubriant

US 3rd ARMY
(Patton)

Angers

Tours
AUG 17

Dijon

F R A N C E

SWITZERLAND

St Nazaire

Nantes

R. Loire

0   50   100   150 km

0   50   100 miles

---

for three days. The following day the British 11th Armoured Division triumphantly entered the port of Antwerp.

ANVIL

While the fighting around Falaise was at its height, a second Allied invasion had taken place in the south of France. On 15 August American and French troops, sailing from Italy, landed on the French Mediterranean coast and were soon advancing up the Rhône Valley against only light opposition from the retreating remnants of the German 19th

Army. The operation – code-named ANVIL and later renamed DRAGOON – was a side-show compared with the D-Day invasion, but, nonetheless, the Franco-American forces captured Lyons and on 11 September linked up with the Americans of 3rd Army.

VICTORY IN EUROPE

At the start of September 1944 the Allies were confident of a speedy victory. It seemed that the war was as good as over and a mood of euphoria reigned. But this illusion was to be quickly shattered. Eisenhower, who had

LYONS

'New Dawn', June 6, 1944 (extract)

The battered shore bleeds, as the littered tidewater recedes,
Leaving the wounded and the dead, washing in a surf that
quickly turned red,
Smoking hulks – carnage – debris; sickening smell from TNT;
Barbed wire – 'Achtung Minen' – poles in the sand; get across
Yank, if you can.

The coastline bled, our sons spilled some, on Omaha Beach to
leave
Buckets of tears shed back home, many mothers forever would
grieve.

What took place in '44, is seldom remembered much anymore,
It was such a long, long time ago, boys forgotten that made it
so,
But mothers, brothers and old Aunt Sue will never forget the
Gray and Blue;
Their faded photos in a bureau drawer, taken back in Devon in
'44.

Like all epic battles this too was won by naive young men
carrying a gun;
Moms' boys and young dads too, willing to die for Red, White
and Blue.
Don't forget them dear people, can't you see, those we left in
Normandy,
Under Crosses and Stars, lined up in rows, all just plain GI Joes.

J. Robert Slaughter, 116th Regiment, 29th US Infantry
Division. The 29th was called the Blue and Gray.

taken over from Montgomery as commander of the Allied armies, at once found himself facing a serious problem of supplies. Fuel, ammunition and stores now had to be transported over long distances from Cherbourg and Arromanches to the troops at the front. The Allied advance was halted to allow supplies to be brought up, and the delay proved to be fatal. The Germans, whose front in the west had virtually disintegrated, were given time to regroup. Fresh units, many of them made up of little more than boys, were scraped together and thrown into the line. By mid-September the German defence was already hardening.

ALLIED SUPPLY CRISIS

The first shock came in the third week of September when a daring attempt by Eisenhower and Montgomery to smash a way across the lower Rhine in Holland ended in failure. Two American airborne divisions and one British were dropped in line ahead to seize three vital bridges. The British 1st Airborne, which was assigned the farthest bridge over the Rhine at Arnhem, landed in an area where elements of two panzer divisions were refitting. The British paratroopers held the bridge but became locked in a bloody struggle with superior German forces. The Allied armour got through to the two American divisions but was unable to relieve the British. After an epic eight day stand against heavy odds, the British division pulled back across the Rhine, leaving more than 7,000 men either dead or taken prisoner. The Arnhem fiasco came as a serious blow to the Allies. The opportunity to outflank the main German defence line by a concentrated thrust through Holland was lost. And the great river barrier of the Rhine remained.

DISASTER AT ARNHEM

Potentially the most dangerous Allied reverse came in mid-December. Hitler, throwing in all his reserves, launched a surprise counteroffensive against General Hodge's American 1st Army in the snowbound forests of the Belgian Ardennes. The

BATTLE OF THE BULGE

Americans, caught unawares, were thrown back more than 96km (60 miles), but their front held firm and after fierce fighting the offensive was broken up. The battle of the Bulge, as it became known, marked the end of Germany's effort to turn the tide in the west.

The war dragged on for four more months until the spring of 1945, when the Allied armies crossed the Rhine and pushed deep into Germany. In early May American and Soviet troops joined hands on the Elbe, while on 4 May Montgomery, now a field marshal, took the surrender of all the German forces in northwest Germany at his headquarters on

Lüneberg Heath. Three days later, in Rheims in northeast France, General Eisenhower accepted the unconditional surrender of the German Reich. Hitler in the meantime had committed suicide in his Berlin bunker. The war in Europe was finally at an end.

The great Anglo-American enterprise that started out as OVERLORD had achieved its final objective. Hitler's Third Reich was brought to its knees and Europe freed at last from the tyranny of Nazi oppression. It had been a long, hard road the Allies had travelled but it brought them in the end to a historic victory. That road began on the beaches of Normandy.

7 MAY: GERMANY SURRENDERS

Above: The liberation of Paris. American infantry march in line down the Champs Elysées in an impromptu victory parade, 27 August 1944.

CHAPTER TWENTY-TWO

The Beaches Today

Right: The granite
obelisk on OMAHA
beach commemo-
rating the Allied
landings on D-Day.
Similar monuments in
English and in French
are to be found at all
the main landing
sites as well as at
Bénouville by the
Pegasus Bridge.

Today, sixty years on, the Normandy countryside shows few signs of the savage fighting that took place in the summer of 1944. The ruined villages have been restored, the city of Caen and the big towns of St Lô and Cherbourg almost totally rebuilt. The coastal villages from Arromanches to Ouistreham are once again thriving resorts packed with holiday-makers throughout the summer months. But the memory of D-Day and the great Allied invasion has been carefully preserved. Along the entire Normandy coast are monuments and 2 museums at Ste. Mère eglise to remind today's visitor of the historic events of sixty years ago.

At UTAH beach on the Cotentin peninsula a commemorative monument on the dunes of La Madeleine marks the spot where the US 4th Infantry Division came ashore. Close by is a display of German and American armour and weapons. Museums depicting the invasion are to be found at Ste Marie-du-Mont, at Cherbourg and at Avranches where the American break out into Brittany took place and Patton's tanks swept through the corridor. While at Ste Mère-Eglise, where a museum commemorates the American air-drop, a hotel has been named after John Steele, the now legendary, most unfortunate American paratrooper whose trapped parachute left him hanging from the church tower on D-Day morning.

The name OMAHA has now been formally adopted by the French for the long sweeping curve of beach where the Big Red One and the 29th Divisions landed. Driving today along the beautiful shore road bordered by luxury villas, gardens and private tennis courts, it is hard to imagine that this was the scene of such terrible carnage. Only the huge yellow stone monuments at each end of the beach testify to the grim struggle that ensued here. But climb the cliff at the eastern end to Colleville-sur-Mer and the picture changes. For here, overlooking OMAHA beach, lies the vast American Cemetery, 70 hectares (172 acres) of landscaped grounds with the graves of more than 9,000 American war-dead. The magnificent white stone memorial comprises a semicircular colonnade with loggias at either end. Inside the loggias, engraved in the stone, are battle maps that illustrate in detail the whole course of the Normandy campaign.

A short distance east of the fishing village

UTAH

STE MERE-EGLISE

OMAHA

COLLEVILLE-SUR-MER

Retrospect (6 June 1944)

It means so much to me, to know that I was here,
Along with men who were no more than boys –
And on that day to share with them unspoken fear,
That in the balance lay life's future joys.

Now, as we stand here old and grey
At this historic battle scene,
Let's pray for those we lost that day –
But ponder how things might have been.

James Hinton, Royal Navy

Left: The remains of Port Winston – the MULBERRY floating harbour off GOLD beach, seen from the cliffs above Arromanches.

POINTE DU HOC

BRITISH BEACHES

MULBERRY

PEGASUS BRIDGE

of Grandcamp a signposted road leads off to the Pointe du Hoc where, on the cliff top, a granite pylon monument marks the place where Colonel Rudder's Rangers scaled the cliffs on D-Day. The German fortifications, most of which remain, still bear the scars of that heroic battle.

The British beaches of GOLD, JUNO and SWORD are less well marked than the American beaches, but there are monuments at Courseulles, Bernières, St Aubin and Ouistreham, and museums at Bayeux, Caen, Riva Bella and Arromanches. In many ways Arromanches is the most evocative of the coastal sites, as just offshore can still be seen many of the concrete caissons of 'Port Winston', the great MULBERRY harbour – an enduring relic of 1944. Further along the coast road, at Luc-sur-Mer, the wicked barrel of an 88-mm gun pokes out of the slit embrasure of a pillbox, a reminder of the bitter resistance put up by the German defenders in Normandy.

By far the best marked of the British invasion sites is the famous Pegasus Bridge

THE 6TH (BRITISH)AIRBORNE DIVISION LANDED NEAR THIS BRIDGE ON THE NIGHT 5TH JUNE 1944 AS A SPEARHEAD OF THE ALLIED ARMIES OF LIBERATION.

LA 6ème DIVISION AEROPORTEE BRITANNIQUE A ATTERRI A PROXIMITE DE CE PONT DANS LA NUIT DU 5 AU 6 JUIN 1944 EN TANT QUE FLECHE DES ARMEES ALLIEES DE LIBERATION.

Right and left: The famous Pegasus Bridge at Bénouville and the fitting commemorative sign. The photograph of the bascule (elevating) bridge over the Orne canal is taken almost from the very spot where Major John Howard's leading glider crash-landed after midnight on D-Day. This, the original historic structure, was dismantled at the end of 1993 to be replaced by a new, heavier road bridge.

Right: The American military cemetery at Colleville-sur-Mer overlooking the eastern end of OMAHA beach.

Left: The memorial colonnade at Colleville with loggias at each end. On the platform is a bronze statue – the 'Spirit of American Youth' – a tribute to those who gave their lives in the Normandy operation. The sculptor was Donald De Lue of New York.

Ranville

I stood alone amidst a crowd
With tear-dimmed eyes, head slightly bowed.
Then, from afar, there came a sound
As from a phantom battle-ground.
With straining ears, I heard a call
And to the ground I saw him fall
With body limp and painful eyes.
Is this the way a soldier dies?
Then through the mist, across the dune,
There came an old familiar tune;
A bugle call from ages past,
But when I raised my eyes at last
A field of crosses came in sight
Of men who fought for what was right.
I saw vague figures standing there,
Heads held down, they stood in prayer.
My eyes were drawn towards a grave.
It was my friend I could not save.

Cyril Crain

over the Caen Canal at Bénouville. Here are both monuments and a museum which tell the story of the daring seizure of the bridge by Major John Howard and his heroic glider force just after midnight on D-Day. Not far from the bridge, on a lane between Colleville Montgomery and Biéville, are the remains of the huge underground fortress – known to the British as HILLMAN – which formed the HQ of the German coastal defence in the SWORD sector. Set 3 km (2 miles) inland from the beach, it proved an almost impregnable

HILLMAN

Left: The inscription on the Rangers' monument on the Pointe du Hoc.

TO THE HEROIC RANGER COMMANDOS
D2RN E2RN F2RN
OF THE 116TH INF.
WHO UNDER THE COMMAND OF
COLONEL JAMES E. RUDDER
OF THE FIRST AMERICAN DIVISION
ATTACKED AND TOOK POSSESSION OF
THE POINTE DU HOC

Right: The Rangers' monument on the Pointe du Hoc looking north. In the foreground is the entrance to part of the underground German fortifications built into the cliff top. There is a visitors' car park and tourist information close by.

Right: Slapton Sands on the Devon coast, looking north. The US 4th Division carried out the rehearsals for the UTAH landing from this part of southern England. It was the scene of the tragic operation TIGER.

Right: A road near GOLD beach honours the British regiment that first landed there. The routes followed by liberating Allied units have been similarly marked all over Normandy.

bastion until stormed late on D-Day by the 1st Battalion of the Suffolk Regiment, to whom there is a moving memorial. Even today the place has a sinister aura. No monument better illustrates the formidable strength of Hitler's Atlantic Wall.

At Merville, east of the Orne, is a memorial to the men of Colonel Otway's 9th Para Battalion who dared all in their capture of the coastal battery. But the most moving testament to the British sacrifice are the gravestones in 16 small cemeteries located along

MERVILLE

CEMETERIES

the line of advance and containing in all more than 19,000 British dead. These cemeteries – the largest of which is in Bayeux – are all superbly maintained by the Commonwealth War Graves Commission. In addition there are six German military cemeteries containing 78,000 graves – a telling reminder of the price the Germans paid for their blind obedience to Adolf Hitler.

ENGLAND

On the other side of the Channel the main British memorial is the popular D-Day Museum at Portsmouth, the city with a naval base from which many of the British assault troops embarked. A principal feature is the

D-DAY MUSEUM

magnificent OVERLORD Embroidery – with 34 detailed panels, the largest of its kind in the world and a colourful depiction of the greatest amphibious invasion in history.

But there is one British beach which holds a place of honour alongside those of Normandy itself. At Slapton Sands near Dartmouth in Devon are two memorials: one erected by the US Army in recognition of the people of the area who abandoned their homes to provide a training ground, the other comprises plaques placed by the British and by the US military to honour the American soldiers who lost their lives in the 'invasion before Normandy' – the ill-fated exercise of Operation TIGER. By their sacrifice they, too, made possible the victory of D-Day.

SLAPTON SANDS

Above: A panel from the magnificent OVERLORD Embroidery at the Portsmouth City Museum, Hampshire. The scene depicts flotillas of the vital Royal Navy minesweepers clearing the channels for the invasion fleet.

Left: A simple commemorative panel at Colleville-sur-Mer.

THINK NOT ONLY UPON THEIR PASSING
REMEMBER THE GLORY OF THEIR SPIRIT

Bibliography

Bradley, Omar N., *A Soldier's Story*, New York, 1951

Bryant, Arthur, *The Turn of the Tide*, London, 1957

Bryant, Arthur, *Triumph in the West*, London, 1959

Churchill, Winston S., *The Second World War*, vols. 4 and 5, London, 1975 and 1976

Cruickshank, Charles, *Deception in World War II*, London, 1979

D'Este, Carlo, *Decision in Normandy*, London, 1983

Eisenhower, Dwight D., *Crusade in Europe*, London, 1948

Gale, Richard, *With the 6th Airborne in Normandy*, London, 1948

Hastings, Max, *Overlord*, London, 1984

Hoyt, Edwin P., *The Invasion Before Normandy*, London, 1987

Irving, David, *The War Between the Generals*, London, 1981

Keegan, John, *Six Armies in Normandy*, London, 1982

Liddell Hart, Sir Basil, *History of the Second World War*, London, 1970

McKee, Alexander, *Caen: Anvil of Victory*, London, 1965

Montgomery, Field Marshal Viscout, *El Alamein to the River Sangro and Normandy to the Baltic*, London, 1973

Paine, Lauren, *D-Day*, London, 1981

Ryan, Cornelius, *The Longest Day*, London, 1960

Shrubb, R.E.A. and Sainsbury, A.B. (Editors), *The Royal Navy Day by Day*, Portsmouth Royal Naval Museum, 1979

Speidel, Hans, *We Defended Normandy*, London, 1951

Tedder, Lord, *With Prejudice*, London, 1966

Tute, Warren, *D-Day*, London, 1974

Wilmot, Chester, *The Struggle for Europe*, London, 1952

Young, Desmond, *Rommel*, London, 1950

Young, Peter, *D-Day*, London, 1981

Index

Photographic Acknowledgments

Archiv für Kunst und Geschichte 12, 24, 25, 71, 100, 101, 106 top, 132; Bildarchiv Preussischer Kulturbesitz 35, 79, 82, 96–97, 98; Derek Blizard 153 bottom; Robert Capa/Magnum 80, 83, 137; Cookworthy Museum 30; Bob Hadley LRPS 153 top; Lieutenant Commander George Honour DSC VRD 64; Hulton Deutsch Collection 17, 26, 38–39, 81, 107, 110, 133; Imperial War Museum 8, 9, 13, 14, 18–19, 21, 27, 29, 31, 33 top, 41, 42, 43, 45, 46, 47, 48, 50, 53, 56–57, 59, 67, 74, 77 top, 87, 88, 89, 93, 94, 95, 97, 106 bottom, 112, 113, 114, 115, 124–125, 127, 142; Imperial War Museum/General Sir John Mogg GCB CBE DSO DL 7; Imperial War Museum/Reed International Picture Library 62–63, 108–109, 111; National Archives 23, 28, 61, 65, 69, 75, 78, 84, 85, 102, 103, 105; National Archives/M. Rudolph Vetter 51, 55; National Archives of Canada 20; Novosti 10; Popperfoto 123; Portsmouth City Council 154–155; Roger-Viollet/ Boyer Viollet 76–77, /Collection Viollet 32, 90–91, 117, /Harlingue Viollet 116, /Lapi Viollet 99, 141, /ND Viollet 145; Süddeutscher Verlag 118, 119, 130–131, 134; Topham Picture Source 14–15, 22, 33 bottom, 49, 52, 54, 60, 126, 129, 139 left, 139 right; Ullstein 86, 136, 138.

Special photography by Richard McConnell 1, 2–3, 147, 148 top, 148 bottom, 149, 150–151, 151, 152 top, 152 bottom, 153 top, 155 bottom.

Acknowledgments

The author wishes to record his appreciation of the help given by members of the British Normandy Veterans' Association and by United States Veterans and Regimental Associations in the compilation of this book. In particular I should like to thank Leonard G. Lomell for his invaluable assistance on points of detail regarding the Pointe du Hoc landing, and George B. Honour for his account of Operation Gambit. I am also indebted to the staff of the BBC's Written Archives for permission to publish extracts from dispatches by BBC War Correspondents, and to Mary Welch, former Reference Librarian of the BBC World Service, for research on my behalf. I wish finally to record my gratitude to the late Tom Baird for his help and encouragement in getting me started.